TIMOTHY JONES

FULLY BELOVED

MEETING GOD IN OUR HEARTACHES AND OUR HOPES

NELSON BOOKS
An Imprint of Thomas Nelson

Fully Beloved

Copyright © 2026 by Timothy Jones

Published by Nelson Books, an imprint of Thomas Nelson, 501 Nelson Place, Nashville, TN 37214, USA. Nelson Books and Thomas Nelson are registered trademarks of HarperCollins Christian Publishing, Inc.

Published in association with the literary agency of Pape Commons, Colorado Springs, CO.

Thomas Nelson titles may be purchased in bulk for educational, business, fundraising, or sales promotional use. For information, please email SpecialMarkets@ThomasNelson.com.

ISBN 978-1-4002-5524-4 (audiobook)
ISBN 978-1-4002-5498-9 (ePub)
ISBN 978-1-4002-5479-8 (TP)

HarperCollins Publishers, Macken House, 39/40 Mayor Street Upper, Dublin 1, D01 C9W8, Ireland (https://www.harpercollins.com)

Library of Congress Cataloging-in-Publication Data

Names: Jones, Timothy, 1995- author
Title: Fully beloved : meeting God in our heartaches and our hopes / Timothy Jones.
Description: Nashville, TN : Thomas Nelson, [2026] | Summary: "Author and pastor Timothy Jones brings into sharp focus one of the most pressing questions of our lives: Am I loved? He offers readers an authentic, intimate, and spiritually nourishing exploration of how God's nature of love really impacts our lives, unlocking our deep healing, our connection with others, and our passion for life"-- Provided by publisher.
Identifiers: LCCN 2025037801 (print) | LCCN 2025037802 (ebook) | ISBN 9781400254798 trade paperback | ISBN 9781400254989 ebook
Subjects: LCSH: Love--Religious aspects--Christianity | God--Love | Christian life
Classification: LCC BV4639 .J64 2026 (print) | LCC BV4639 (ebook)
LC record available at https://lccn.loc.gov/2025037801
LC ebook record available at https://lccn.loc.gov/2025037802

Cover design: Studio Gearbox
Cover illustration: marukopum / Shutterstock
Interior Design: Kristy Edwards

Printed in the United States of America

25 26 27 28 29 LBC 5 4 3 2 1

CONTENTS

The ache of the human heart has always been to be made whole.

—Jeff Crosby

PROLOGUE

AM I LOVED? MAYBE NO QUESTION NAGS AT US MORE. Perhaps no question matters as much. We need meaningful connection with others, now more than ever, when loneliness is, as a public health official said, epidemic, when the world seems more fractured. Some of us miss a closeness we once had. Or long for what we sense we could have. For we see that at its core, living means relating. Even a small gesture reminds us of that: A barista's upbeat comment gives our day a lift. Or a bigger gift comes. A friend writes a note to thank us for the courage we showed in taking a stand. Someone we hurt says, "I forgive you." A loved one's face, lit by the glow of candlelight, turns toward us with affection. Who doesn't feel buoyed up by such moments, these reminders that we are cared for?

Relationships can also be complicated, of course. Even bewildering. A single misunderstanding can cut deeply. Some of us grew up hearing voices that said, "You need to prove yourself." Maybe someone you love rejects you, writes you out of their life, as happened to me. A remembered cruel comment may leave us aching for assurance. Encounters like these remind us of how easily we forget our worth. What a gift it would be to truly recover that conviction! We long to know that healing happens, that broken things will mend. And we'd like an alternative to the polarizing conversations and drifting apart. For we sense more is possible.

While the affection others give matters profoundly, it will only meet us partway. Human tenderness alone will not—cannot—satisfy our deepest selves. We need a sturdier, more lasting love—one that comes from the Maker of all things, a God we hope will overflow in kindness. I believe that our emotional distancing and division spring from uncertainty here and from the sense that we still haven't found what our hearts are searching for.

Seeing others experience that kind of life-giving love—and feeling it grow in me—has triggered a seismic shift: from feeling underloved to discovering new joy.

The glory of God is a person fully alive, as the ancient sage Irenaeus put it. It's clearer to me than ever that such aliveness comes from knowing I am more beloved than I thought. I'm less alone than I feared. I can let go of the shame. Grace will meet me in the guilt I feel for things done or left undone. A God of kindness shows up right where I live, to the world where we all live.

What I write in these pages points to the discoveries I've made in reading Scripture and wise voices in my Christian tradition. Ancient wisdom from the likes of Augustine or Julian of Norwich has given me a lot to ponder and pray about. And in the searching questions of a poet like Emily Dickinson I'm seeing something ageless and compelling. More contemporary voices, too, leave me grateful for their insights. I've been exploring convictions we need right now, ancient truth that seems as current as today's news feed. As you read, I hope that you sense, as I have, something special at work in the world and glimpse how you could share in it.

And what if we could experience such love overflowing from our lives into those of others? A new conviction of our being treasured by God could push out the competition and striving that make it harder to live with the people next door. Believing that God values us deeply makes us more able to love others, not less.

But then, we may wonder or worry there too. Questions may

trouble our relationship with God. Some mornings at least, God seems far removed. Does God care enough, notice me enough, to meet me in daily life? My friend Seawell once said, "Growing up, God was 'up there' and I was just Seawell 'down here.' There was a distance. I couldn't imagine feeling close." Would God even want to hear us talk?

But my friend also had a hunch that more was possible.

In my account of what I'm discovering, I tell personal stories that have shaped my understanding. Some of these moments are painful, some funny, some simple in their beauty. Though these stories arise from my life, please don't think they are just about me. The most personal thing we tell often turns out to be the most universal. I feel an urgency to tell relatable stories. I will share others' discoveries too. It gets a little intense, but I decided you can grasp something as big as God's love only by setting it in the midst of our everyday stresses and relational messes.

And I hope that these accounts will inspire you to reflect on your own life. I write as the pastor I am, as an author who cares deeply about our contemporary culture with its aches and longings. I believe that what others have shown me as they stumble through the depths and valleys or scale the heights bears repeating.

I wonder: How is God present *for you*? Where in your heartaches and hopes does that presence become known? Does God see our pains, know we are lonely, and want to hold us close? What if God loves us—already—more than we can fathom?

These are questions I'd love to help you explore. For might there open up before us and in us a more satisfying friendship with God? A deepened conviction of our own belovedness?

I've been finding it can happen, and in a surprising place. In the Trinity I'm seeing that God assures us that we are known and loved. All three persons—Father, Son, and Holy Spirit—come close. They meet us in transforming ways. I've long known that believers, ancient and contemporary, have found in such language utter delight. Which leads me to believe that we, too, find hope in this portrait of God. Through decades of pastoring and praying, grieving and wrestling, I realize that love is the startling invitation of the Trinity and the extravagant answer to the most pressing questions of my own life.

Yes, the very word *Trinity* for some might seem difficult and complicated and even off-putting. But what if this venerable belief points to a God whose very nature has to do with rich relationship? Talk of the Trinity, I'm becoming convinced, will warm our times with God, not complicate them. There's a surprising intimacy when you look closely. Father, Son, and Holy Spirit radiate and overflow with beauty and splendor and kindness.

Couldn't we find great relief there? In our brokenness and loneliness, God—whose nature is love—knows us and cares for us. A new freedom around God becomes ours. Mercy shows up in ways we wouldn't imagine.

My prayer is to know better God's embracing grace found in such a picture. That you will too. May this book be a hopeful gift. It will become, I pray, your summons to a whole and joyful life. Your invitation to a new conviction that you are fully beloved.

ONE

WHAT IF LOVE GHOSTS US?

So much of my life has been spent fruitlessly searching for the missing piece of my own interior jigsaw.

—Elizabeth Callen

The single desire that dominated my search for delight was simply to love and to be loved.

—Saint Augustine

I CAN'T RECALL WHERE I WAS WHEN I OPENED MY MOTHER's letter—my grad school dorm on Alexander Street, maybe—but I'm sure that by the second paragraph I'd sat down.

"Send us back your house key," her neat handwriting read.

So, I thought, *she's speaking for both her and my dad.* The return address on the envelope was my childhood home in coastal California. "You are not," she went on, "welcome in our house."

Telling them my plans to marry had already prompted a stream of letters, all in my mom's unhesitating script, letters that told of their vision of me finishing at Princeton and *then,* and *only then*, thinking about a serious relationship. Their letters came to me, their youngest son—an overprotected young person who lived at home while at college—convinced that surely I couldn't be ready for a lifelong commitment. And yes, at twenty-one I *was* young. I can understand why they might have a question or two.

But to have my parents write me out of the family? They not only disapproved but they also refused to meet Jill, the person I deeply loved and wanted to marry.

"If in a few years you come to your senses, then maybe we will talk," my mother wrote. "But don't approach us. We will contact you." Talk about rejection!

The request for my house key was for effect, I realize; they didn't need my little slab of door lock–shaped metal, and they knew where I lived—the Princeton street where they'd sent the letter. But the words hit their mark.

Another letter followed, hinting they'd write me out of their will. But the warning injected into the stream of my mother's letters was clear: stir up fear, go for drama, dangle an inheritance. A hazard hung in the air. If I were to go through with my plans, the latest letter intimated, I'd be unwelcome, disinvited. The message: *Maybe you aren't one of us after all.*

When I look back, I see Mom pressing for a showdown, setting herself up for a letdown—and putting me in a hard place. Life-changing letters like those force tough choices.

Whatever path I went down, life would be forever different.

I never sent the key. My parents never raised the request again, for reasons I will explain later. I could feel the loss I was facing, to be sure, but my heart was racing ahead to the gleaming chance to spend a lifetime of companionship with my best friend.

STRAINING FOR CONNECTION

Many of us are struggling to stay connected, trying to hold on to our relationships while forces pull us apart. One writer called this era "The Anti-Social Century," marked by growing loneliness.[1] Some of our solitude is self-imposed. We've gotten out of the habit of nurturing friendship and rich family connections. Sometimes we drift apart. An annoying uncle means we fall out of the habit of having family get-togethers. Family members may support us and keep us going or put us on the defensive. A good-sized number of American adults say they're estranged from their mothers—and even more from their fathers. Some people are choosing to cut off toxic parents and go "no contact." We can end up feeling alone all kinds of ways. Whether in unwanted silences, our own busyness, or middle-of-the-night wonderings, many of us experience a lonely restlessness.

And our life's rejections—small and almost forgotten or still looming large—affect us over the years. Our heart feels tender-sore instead of tenderly held. Some of us gingerly navigate a walk-on-your-tiptoes relationship. Or I wonder how the threat of losing another's love might leave you worried and wilting.

We've gotten out of the habit of nurturing friendship and rich family connections. Sometimes we drift apart.

And while many of our rejections are not as dramatic as mine with my parents, we may struggle with our standing with others, what some call status anxiety. We worry we've somehow missed being granted a certificate of belonging. Maybe there was a bully at school whose humiliations still leave us seething or ashamed all these years later. (One woman, still stinging, wrote of reconnecting through social media, years later, with some of her "mean girl" peers. And she told a story of the relational healing she found.)

I think of a woman I know who met with a demand for a separation. Her husband sat her down, divorce papers in hand, claiming, "You haven't been enough." What a blow! Or we face other absences. Essayist and poet Maggie Smith, in the wake of a split, spending that dreaded holiday morning without her children, wrote, "It was my second Christmas since my marriage ended but my first Christmas morning without my kids—the first time they weren't here overnight on Christmas Eve. . . . [Going for a run in the neighborhood], I did my best to outrun my sadness."[2] As a friend of mine put it, thinking of his young children and the pressures they face, the perils they navigate as a family, "I feel the world is a cold place, and it's easy to spiral into loneliness."

Or maybe a friend ghosts us—dropping out from a text thread, leaving messages unanswered, leaving us with cool silence as a substitute for connection. We wonder: *Was it something I said?* Or maybe a church makes us feel unwelcome. You walk into a foyer or parish hall, only to watch clumps of longtime friends close ranks, their laughter and stories walling you out. You stand there awkwardly, worse than invisible.

Or there might be the cascading micro-rejections when strangers are randomly rude—because of how you look or where you came from or simply for your being who you are. And, of course, we've all seen how political discussion can turn personal in poisonous or toxic ways. Conversation becomes a field of combat. We may feel attacked.

I'm talking about the ache of missing out—on the belonging, the community, the life we sense we were created for.

No wonder we long for something we barely glimpse but also believe is possible. But how do you maintain a certainty of being beloved when voices tell you that you aren't worthy? When people wield shame-throwers? When your soul cries out?

The details of my story—any story about love and loss—may look different from yours, but we all come from families with complicated attachments. The love others offer us can be, by turns, exhilarating and confusing. We do well to be honest about that, for we worry about love, wonder over it. We long for it and often grasp for it. Or maybe the one we care so much about is lukewarm toward us, and we suffer with the indifference. Sometimes even joyfully intimate relationships suffer flat stretches.

Experiences like these might be opening you up to something more, something deeper and better—just as they have for me.

LOVE BEYOND CLICHÉ

If you have read this far, some part of you is seeking something. Wherever we come from, whatever our varied experiences, life is, at least some days, harder than we want. The things we cherish—favorite gifts, proudest achievements, closest friendships—can fade or fall apart. Or at least lose some luster.

I reflect on that time with my parents, the letters that came, an ugly encounter later with Mom on a sidewalk near my home that seared even more. I'm still working on what it means to be loved and to love when life's no stroll.

My parents' rejection was hard to take, but it also stirred a longing. "When you lose someone you love," wrote Maggie Smith, reflecting on the pain of her broken marriage, "you start to look for new ways to understand the world."[3] Maybe you've been here too: searching for a love that feels more secure. You know the pain when harsh words from others get stuck on replay in your mental playlist, making it hard to believe you're truly accepted—that you aren't an imposition on the world's comings and goings.

And perhaps it's in these hard moments—or dull, routine stretches—that we're being readied for deeper connection, for a clearer view of the world, and for a closer relationship with the one who made it all. Can you think of times your longings made your heart restless, as Augustine put it, until it found its rest in God? I mean maybe times when pressures kneaded you hard but in the end made you able to rise? The harshness led not to despair but to discovery?

Perhaps it's in these hard moments—or dull, routine stretches—that we're being readied for deeper connection, for a clearer view of the world, and for a closer relationship with the one who made it all.

Such language runs the risk of cliché. I mean by *belovedness* more than what Frederick Buechner referred to as "a cozy emotional feeling."[4] I'm picturing more than a self-centered, self-enclosed warmth. More than surface pleasantness. I mean something more durable. Love becomes more than emotion but also a rock-steady decision for the good of the other.

This isn't simply a wavelet of self-acceptance or the trendy notion of "self-care." I picture something more powerful, more lasting—something that runs through us like our lifeblood, not just a shallow feeling. An artery, not a capillary. I mean meeting God in a deeper encounter—a God who, in my tradition, is the source of life and love. Whose affection can be trusted.

Glimpsing that we are cherished in this way offers a promise amid the normal—and not-so-normal—setbacks. Our hesitant steps gain momentum as we move toward the radiant source of life and love. When God invites us into a life-giving relationship, doesn't it free us from the need to always defend ourselves?

Not that Christians have always played up—or even shown in daily acts—this loving dimension of God. Pious people aren't always the best advertisement for the faith. But I'm discovering that God's closeness calms what feels frantic. Agitation gets replaced with new assurance.

When God invites us into a life-giving relationship, doesn't it free us from the need to always defend ourselves?

Julian of Norwich, the medieval pray-er I'll say more about later, enlisted a great word common in her time for what I'm describing: *dearworthy*. It means prized. Priceless. Julian applied it to Jesus—how he becomes dear to us when we see him give his life at great sacrifice. But again and again she also applied *dearworthy* to us, pointing to God's endearing eternal fondness for you and me that makes *us* so. We hold tight to the promise that, in Christ, God sees us as beloved. If we could realize more deeply how God's love overcomes the aches of the human heart, what a difference we'd see in us and others would see in us!

WEATHERING THE WORST

Exploring questions like "Am I loved?" or "Does God care?" is a lifetime's work. It's also an everyday challenge. For taking in the love at the heart of things helps us weather the worst that relationships throw at us. We begin to find an alphabet, a generous pile of words, an *entire book* to explore such depths, to use an image from poet Emily Dickinson. "We learned," she wrote, "the Whole of Love."[5] It is, as she called it, a mighty book indeed. We open a volume to which we keep coming back, like a good story we read and reread. A story that leaves us with new angles each time.

And maybe here is a possibility of a new chapter for you, when in your life story you've heard a shaming voice accuse, "You don't measure up." Perhaps you would normally run to your self-improvement lists and goal charts. You try to fix yourself, hoping you might avoid being overlooked or forgotten. But over time, when challenges drag on, hope can fade. You feel worn down by how cold and impersonal the world can be.

But then, even when we feel the cuts and jabs, feel swamped by circumstances, we sense the presence of something bigger, sweeter. Someone close by. Beyond our imagining, in our hearts we are *met.* God comes to us, ready with words like *dearworthy*, *cherished*, *invited*. A Presence draws near—one who nourishes the soul, even with its insecurities and intensities.

And then you and I can more clearly see how genuine love begins to lift us above the pain of rejection or a request to return a house key. Love does not so much measure us as treasure us. Something within settles when we realize God offers us grace, in spite of who we are *not*, and in all the ways we fall flat on our face. Here, mercy overcomes our very real sense of having let God and others down.

Might this kindness not help us when others fail us, allowing us to move through and beyond envy and blaming? The space inside us feels bigger, more spacious, more able to make room for others and their failings. We discover how we may find what it takes to give more to others than we ever could on our own. This is no Hallmark movie where we hear sketchy advice to just "follow your heart." This love is grittier in the best way. This affection feels more transcendent. More enduring.

And so, what might seem merely spiritual becomes wonderfully practical, working itself out in the scenes of everyday life.

THE RECKONING WE ALL FACE

These days I ask myself: How did that letter—asking for the return of a key—trigger a spiritual reckoning that still shapes me? In some ways those ghosting letters were nudging me to an even more urgent, ever-deepening fascination with a God of love.

People seem surprised to hear me say how much the picture of God found in Father, Son, and Holy Spirit warms our view of God. They picture that talk of the Trinity only clutters our view of God. Why complicate the faith's simple message? Can't we just say, "God loves us"? Isn't that enough? And if we get too specific about theological points, don't we run the risk of getting the details wrong? Falling into a heresy that pushes a kind of cosmic "oops" button? So maybe we hold back, or don't try much.

It doesn't have to work that way. I hope to show that if God reveals himself to be wonderfully near, then his ancient conviction about the one and three persons isn't just for the philosophers. It's not about confusing math. Instead, I'm seeing how it's an extraordinary invitation to taste the compassion we've always longed for, the mercy we've secretly hoped could cover us. Rather than wearying or wearing down our minds, pondering this picture of God fortifies our emotional resources. We then have more to give others, not less. I see it not as an abstract formulation but a living portrait saturated with communal richness. A glimpse of joy overflowing, spilling into ordinary and extraordinary moments.

Such language woven into the Bible's stories and soaring passages grounds our conversation about God—and our talking *to* God—in the fertile soil of the personal. It can be a way to meet a God who, we see again and again in Scripture, stands ready for real connection. It points to a God who will go to any length, including the suffering of a cross, to invite us back to fellowship and engage us in community. It can feel poignant, when you plumb the story. And stubbornly hopeful.

This portrait of God can seem complex or arcane when you stumble into the theological weeds of a seminary textbook. I do see a place for a few weighty tomes, by the way, like those on my own bookshelves. Were you to see my home study's crowded bookcases, you might wonder if my quest has become an obsession. But at their best such works make a simple point about God's nature. The theologian and the pastor point us to an unimaginably vast being who still offers us richness and relationship. And such lofty heights have much to do with our everyday depths. The infinite becomes intimate.

I think of the most personal aspects of human experience: a parent and child, a loving spouse, a conversation within the family. And yes, these scenes from real human life give us imperfect word pictures. We understand them as only partial. But they give us appropriate foretastes of a wider, greater glory. For if another person's love—that of a parent or friend or spouse—can flood us with tenderness and coax from us joyful tears, why would it be a stretch to speak of a God as helping us in a similar way? Our pictures and faltering words can't compare to the genuine, eternal article, but they get us started, whet our appetites, and fan our yearnings.

WORKING THE WORRY BEADS

An assurance of being fully beloved continues to draw me—and elude me. The prospect is like a few of those books on my shelf, well-worn from use, dog-eared, perhaps with a spine showing signs of wear: a volume I keep coming back to, seeing passages I've marked in the margins, but this time with a new question or some urgency in mind. A friend likened this kind of question to a string of worry beads, common in the Middle East, carried in your pocket or purse. You pull it out to help you think with greater clarity and calmness.

I traveled to England with such questions rolling around in my mind, a week that would form part of my sabbatical from my position as senior minister and dean of a downtown cathedral. One of my stops, I had hoped, would be a meeting with the renowned

Rowan Williams, now-retired Master of Magdalene College in Cambridge—a kind of Gandalf of the scholarly world. A friend of mine who happened to know the venerable scholar and former Anglican archbishop sent him a message about me. A meeting was set up.

I sat there, taking in the titles of books packed tightly on his floor-to-ceiling shelves, some even spilling onto the floor (and I thought *I* had a library-load of books). I told Rowan how I wanted to express what I'd come to believe about God—the relationship and intimacy possible there, even amid our human brokenness and divisions. I shared parts of my life and how the Trinity seems to speak to that longing to be seen and known. I pulled out my journal, where I'd jotted questions I'd been wrestling with. A worry bead or two, indeed.

As we spoke I noticed—amid the books and files—icons, scenes of saints, and portraits of Jesus himself, adding to the ambience. I sat in the presence of not only impressive intellect but also winsome piety. And under his bushy white brows, I saw a glimmer of warmth. What Rowan said affected me more than he could know: "If God is relational," he supposed out loud, "there can be no thing in God's creation that is not somehow embedded in relationship." Including us. Of course—a personal, accessible God *would* leave traces in all creation. Everywhere, all the time.

And vastly more than traces. "We may be convinced we've been abandoned," he went on. (I could relate, given my ordeal with my parents: I *had been* abandoned. Perhaps you can imagine your own experience or fear of abandonment as you picture my conversation.) But, no, he insisted, we live in a universe where relationships interweave and find harmony. Amid creation's variety, things interlock in a beauty of ordering, to paraphrase another theologian I would discover.[6] And all God's creatures interrelate, constantly interacting.

All we see in the array of living things forms part of a cosmic chorus of praise—even, as the prophet Isaiah said, the trees in the field clapping their hands.[7] And we human beings, the "crown of creation," as the theologians sometimes call us, all the more![8] Even with all the pressures that pull us apart, the toxic messages littering our internet byways, we are part of some larger whole, a wider world, a supreme confraternity. No wonder we are irresistibly social creatures; our identity grows from relational riches. This dimension feeds inescapably into who we've been, who we are, what we hope to become.

With all these interconnections, then, we never feel satisfied with the shallows of human affection. That was part of our conversation too. *Yes,* I thought, scrawling notes in my journal, even as I let Rowan's words catch fire inside. *Maybe I'm not trying in vain to unearth new depths of experiencing God.* I felt internal sparks—not the kind you get from crossed wires, but from a connection that lights something up and makes it work. Here was hope for the brokenness of human life. An expectancy of profound love. *How might we then live—and love—more fully?*

I realized with a new delight that the relationality in all things had roots in the Trinity, grew out of an intimate relating in God's own being. The apostle Paul, so soon after Jesus' coming, death, and resurrection, could write of the "grace of the Lord Jesus Christ, the love of God, and the communion of the Holy Spirit."[9] Paul pictured all that richness as part of our lives.

Or I'd found later voices, like Julian of Norwich, exulting, "The Trinity suddenly filled my heart full of the utmost joy, and I understood that it will be like that in heaven forever for all those who will come there . . . and the Trinity is our unending joy and bliss."[10] Or Catherine of Siena, bursting out, "You, oh eternal Trinity, are a deep Sea, into which the deeper I enter the more I find, and the more I find the more I seek."[11]

Didn't this tack Rowan offered mean that the persons of the Trinity—the Father, the Son (Jesus), the Holy Spirit—show us what love looks like? There is debate about how much we know and can say about God's intra-Trinitarian relating. We see through a glass dimly, darkly. But these voices point to how we might more deeply experience love in all its depths and heights.

And now I could glimpse how the everyday stuff of relating—the raptures, the painful ruptures—ties into our struggles with love. Clearly, these human examples are *not* adequate analogies. It's not that I look at human love and figure out something about how God relates. Let me be clear: Any way in which we picture human love will always feel Gollum-pale and paper-thin next to the divine version. Our best efforts will land far from the divine's inexhaustible depths.

But maybe this picture of Father, Son, and Spirit has more possibilities than we thought. What we experience in relationships with others points to something higher. For here, if we believe what the early church's great minds concluded, we see an *eternal* love made real and close. We see it as God makes, Christ sustains, and the Spirit helps. In this triune portrait we learn something astonishing: "The doctrine of the Trinity is," as Fleming Rutledge wrote, "a working out" of what the New Testament means when it says that God is love. "It tells us that God is love within his own three-personed self, and he is love toward us."[12]

Here the imagination stretches. And the heart leaps. Love, as the love of the Father, the Son, and the Holy Spirit for one another, also entails God's loving self-giving to others. The divine becomes personified yet not bound by the fluctuations of human affections or the strictures of time.

And while this may seem a small point, there's something here, great minds have concluded, that has to do with all time and eternity. I think of ancient prayers I say in church or most mornings, calling God *eternal* Father. If God is everlastingly Father, doesn't it follow there's always been a Son in relationship from before the beginning of it all? And that, from before time and at the foundation of all we see, there is love?

I think often about the encounter with Rowan, recalling how he helped confirm a conviction: While our human loves are pitiably slight versions of divine love, all kinds of love, at their richest moments, prime us to better understand the love of God.

Speaking of England (and on that trip I went not only to Cambridge but also to Oxford), I've been struck lately by an insight from Charles Williams, one of the Oxford Inklings alongside C. S. Lewis and J. R. R. Tolkien. Charles Williams said the passionate longing we have for another person—or feel *from* another—testifies to our desire *for God.* Some of the same synapses activate in both cases.

Yes, I was thinking, *Williams is on to something*: An impassioned longing for someone can be, he said, "a gateway to divine things."[13] Perhaps that thought also helps us to imagine how love in our earthly lives points to a larger love. It now doesn't seem so hard to see how the longing of human love, the desire to belong, points to something greater.

We see how familial love—even with its sad mess-ups—can condition us for a higher love. And yes, the imperfect kind we might experience from parents becomes a resource in meeting God in expectation. And romantic love—pointing beyond itself, beyond the object and subject of our affection, this delighted love Jill and I felt—seemed to be deepening me. It still is.

Even the rejection that tempts us to despair may at the same time open us up, if, as a friend said to me, "it is the intersection of our own stories and our big beliefs where the interesting stuff is found." Picking around in the archaeological digs of normal human life—the stuff of ordinary days, the unspooling hours of sometimes bruising, maybe tedious, and occasionally exhilarating relating—I began to find wild promise in a no-longer-musty belief, one that excites my soul and my heart.

WHEN FATHERS FAIL

I recognize a difficulty right off, though. I need to say, dear reader—perhaps wounded reader—that I realize talk of a relational God, especially couched in the language of fatherly approach, will make some wary. The parental language, for many, will rouse some disturbing memories. "One of Emily [Dickinson's] objections to God," someone wrote of the poet, "is that he is too much like her father."[14]

Such sensitivities may especially crowd around the Christian belief in Jesus' painful last days before his crucifixion. Some argue that what happened on the cross comes off as a betrayal of what a loving heavenly Father should be. There's certainly pain and brokenness here: Jesus' pierced-by-a-spear abdominal side spills out blood and water while he's nailed to the crossbeams. It takes stomach to look on it.

Did Jesus himself experience something akin to the ultimate abandonment? I'd argue not—but he *did* cry to God, "Why have you forsaken me?"[15] If you are like me, you might see, when looking closely, some pretty intense drama. Some pretty high stakes. "Jesus meek and mild" doesn't quite fit the life he lived or the trauma he endured. More like Someone vigorous and a little wild. A building suspense makes the story rattling, when we do more than give a quick glance. What do we make of a heavenly Father who looked on and allowed it to happen?

And when we think about our own lives, what if our dad or mom wasn't kind? What if they were hurtful, even abusive? That wasn't exactly my experience, but my dad was sometimes distracted and distant. It left me with insecurities that still push me to scramble for approval or affirmation from others. I understood what a friend meant when he talked about his dad, who was successful in his publishing career. "He was someone to be proud of," my friend said, "but not someone I really knew." Wouldn't it matter if the story of the Trinity actually took that kind of deep, painful reality seriously?

Why wouldn't we, though, hunt for the acceptance we missed early on? I'm struck by James K. A. Smith; he wrote movingly of "the trauma of being abandoned by a father and then a stepfather, a line of fathers who left." I see why talk of God's father-like love would have piqued his interest. But even so, when he heard it, he recalled, "I still carried a story of abandonment in my gut. The problem [was] . . . a painful wound on the register of my imagination."[16]

I have to admit, a distant or absent dad can tarnish the imagery of "our Father." The same goes for a mother who gave us a diet of relational gruel, leaving us emotionally malnourished. My own mother's presence and absences—her pull-near and push-away parenting—have left me with mixed feelings when I've thought about God's "parenting."

And not only parental caregivers shoulder responsibility for a heart's wounded lameness, a soul's reticence around God: uncles, cousins, blood relations. I think of loveless households or abusive caregivers, the trauma of living with icily distant spouses. The Bible (in the books of Isaiah and Hosea) imagines God as an attentive husband too. But what if your spouse has been unfaithful? Family imagery stirs up stuff.

But might not there be a place to ask, Where did we *get* the sense of how things in a family or from a parent *should* be? What if our very expectation—love as healthy and life-giving and freeing—comes from a true reality at the heart of the universe? My friend Daniel Shepherd had a kind and involved father. "Couldn't the hurtful outcomes some experience—like those of any bad relationship," he once said to me, "send us out looking even more eagerly for the real thing?"

The genuine article might awaken in us a hunger for the true substance when we realize that "the failed version was only a shadow or distorted parody." Some of my quest—and my guess is it's yours too—has to do with undoing harm done, washing clean some of the images sullied by inevitable human failings. So yes, life with a lousy parent: It scars. But what if we could be *re*parented, restored in the wounded places, the invisible, lingering bruises? We could encounter—or maybe even stumble upon—our own souls' healing.

THE HARDSCRABBLE TRUTH

Because the eternal life of God bears on the mundane and grubby particulars of every life, the sorrows as well as the highs, I'm eager to catch signs of the fellowship of the three showing up where I live and, if I may, where you live too.

What follows in the coming chapters is personal and vulnerable. I don't want to overdo the life-story revelations. But the last thing the world needs is another book of spiritual platitudes or vague truths, detached from everyday struggles. I have to tie what I believe or question or long to experience to something true. It has to have some relationship to life's hardscrabble stuff.

When I think about my own desires to pray and draw closer, I picture a way of talking about God and speaking to God that resembles a family's moments of intimacy. That guides my approach. And so, whatever your realities of loss or distance or indifference, I still believe family imagery gives us a grammar for the expansive, extravagant love of God.

And I'm reminded by a mentor like Augustine that even our childhoods—our earliest moments and days—carry clues to what we most long for. Often it is the small and seemingly simple. In considering and perhaps sharing with others the scenes of our relating and lurching and reconciling, might we together see how intimacy and absence, fullness and heartbreak, become, as we grow, dialogue partners with what we believe?

One more orienting point. Because there's more to discover than what we get from newsfeed headlines, podcasts, or the celebrity of the day, I want to include older, tested voices in the conversation—voices who speak of their spiritual discoveries. I place my own unfolding questions and glimpses against the backdrop of older figures who speak into where I live now.

I call on Augustine as a witness, for instance. He lived and taught during a time when early Christianity was both dismissed by cultural elites and beginning to gain great traction. He was deeply moved by the mystery (and misery) of being human: how childhood shapes us, how we stray from the good, and how we can find something deeper than mere self-knowledge.

This has made me wonder: Could other ancient voices—like Julian of Norwich, who lived through plague and chaos—offer wisdom and comfort for our time? She felt a deep love from the Trinity, even in all the sorrow. And in response, she fell deeply in love with the Trinity. I see in her someone not simply interested in theology but devoted, passionate, drenched in joyful longing.

How might that happen for you and me? In their deepening enjoyment of God, what led them to turn often to the rich language of family and household as they grasped for metaphors? I can't help being struck by the contrast—when, for many of us, talk of the Trinity doesn't juice us much or even feels off-putting. Yet even a socially challenged poet like Emily Dickinson, penciling searing images, has moved me. What did they discover? I haven't stopped searching for an answer.

And sometimes, to explore a truth or turn a corner, you mine a story. Maybe your own quiet, even painful story. At times I'll share vignettes from my life—or from theirs—as a way to put flesh on what might otherwise seem hopelessly lofty.

Such epiphanies may greet you in all kinds of settings. You find an image that startles you in a verse of poetry. (I've found more than

I thought I would in Emily Dickinson's letters and poems.) Or you get caught up in the lyrics of a pop song or hymn or oil painting. You discover, as I did, that a nursery ballad or a children's book of prayers you kept all these years now gives new clues. You go along not expecting much, and suddenly you feel brave to look at the interplay of your daily life with holy, heavenly things. You get a better sense of the divine Three accompanying us through.

WHEN TRAUMA STAYS HIDDEN

Some traumas we experience in life involve blood or a broken collarbone or a lost limb. My big loss was quieter than that, more hidden. I didn't see it coming. I wonder what effect that loss of parental blessing ultimately has meant. What it would have felt like not to have to forfeit it.

A part of me, against all reason, looked out on the church folks gathered on that humid May afternoon for our exchange of vows, half-thinking Mom and Dad might have relented and decided, after all, to come. Their presence would have mattered. They were welcome. But they stayed away. There was a finality in my parents' boycott of our wedding. They could never go back in time and be there.

How would I navigate the leaving behind not just to marry but also to break with a parental connection? In the early years of our marriage, I felt embarrassed by the ways my parents had pushed me away. It seemed easier simply not to talk about it much. But already there were clues for how still to flourish. "Where you go, I will go," the minister read for the ceremony in that Pennsylvania church, lifting words from the Hebrew book of Ruth, words Jill and I were saying to *each other*. All the more important, given what we would lose. Here the ancient young woman in the story says to her mother-in-law, "Where you lodge, I will lodge; your people shall be my people, and your God my God."[17] The minister meant it as a reminder: Our home would from now on locate, more than any place or setting, wherever the other was.

As we drove away, I had trouble keeping my eyes on the road and off Jill, who dozed in the passenger seat on that humid late afternoon. Sometimes I held her warm hand, my free arm guiding the wheel. *This is my wife next to me,* I thought. We were together, delighting in married love.

I recall how Christmases those first few years would, with all the customary jubilation, include melancholy, the sense of something lost. Mom and Dad were not only withholding blessing but yanking back the affection we had shared for my years growing up. It took some doing to accept. But you do. We did.

Where would this risky step take us? Wherever, we would not be alone. We would be accompanied—by each other, and by a larger Another.

YOUR BIG INVITATION

There's a finality to having someone seem to write you out of their life. Still, I longed for relationship so deeply that I kept writing my parents. I wanted to keep the channels open—letters about my first job as pastor of a church, the garden we inherited at the parsonage, updates on little Abram's progress as an infant. Something in me sensed that these conduits were too important to ignore.

Would they respond? And on their side, would something soften?

There's more to the story to tell. If you recall your own experience of someone pushing you away, I hope you found some reconciling forces at work. Do you see in God's love for you a way to hang in there when relationships get hard?

As important as the hope for healing is, our reconciliations in this life are always incomplete—partial and fragmented, never fully whole. Sometimes we must endure a broken relationship for a long time, negotiating the pain that surrounds it. Or the shame that comes from rejection. And sometimes we work through the hard, hard severing that happens through the death of a loved one.

But I also want to believe, even more deeply, that what I witness in God as nurturing parent, God as companion on the human road, God as accompanying Spirit, can help our view of God. We might see something anew, take courage, when we try to make sense of the swings the world takes at us, the times of pained isolation, the times we cry out for something more. Nothing less than joy is what I'm seeing ahead—and seeking. My gut tells me it will be worth tending to that longing to be met by God. Worth following the questions, like the ones I'll grapple with in these pages. And worth hoping for more as a divine Other draws near and we see ourselves invited to come close too.

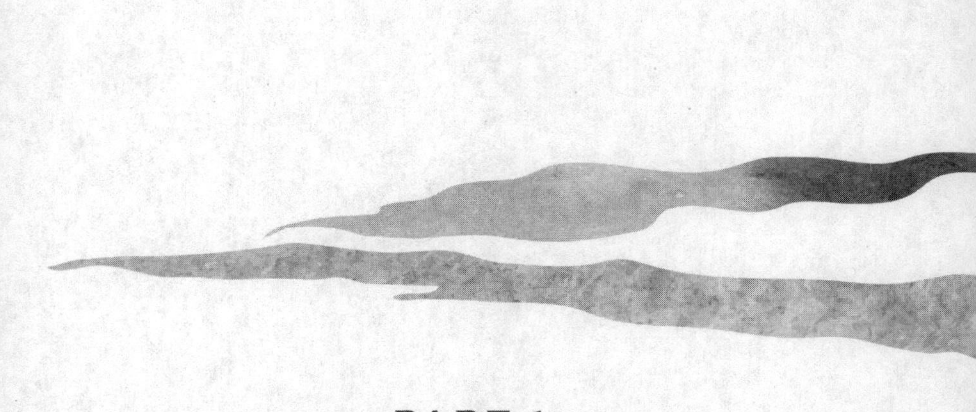

PART 1

OUR GOD MAKES: THE FATHER

TWO

WHO USHERED ME INTO THIS MESSY EXTRAVAGANCE?

I scarcely know where to begin, but love is always a safe place.

—Emily Dickinson

My sadness will be held by someone.

—Morgan Harper Nichols

Love is why we are here at all.

—Anne Lamott

LOTS OF US KNOW SOMETHING OF OUR ORIGIN STORIES—circumstances surrounding our earthly advent.

My brother, Kevin, always insisted that I owe my existence to his pleading. "If it weren't for me," he claimed, mostly serious, "you wouldn't be here."

He badgered Mom and Dad, the story goes, for a brother or sister. He was like a tiny salesman with plaintive eyes and a big ask: a *sibling.* He could be annoyingly sure of himself as an adult, and I suspect the picture was more complicated than all that. Did our parents really need a five-year-old to convince them to have another?

But maybe they did.

I found out, as an adult, that Mom had a miscarriage before I came along—a daughter. No one talked about it, not when I was growing up, their loss kept as a buried family secret, but now I wonder: *Did that sorrow make our parents extra cautious?* I can't imagine Kevin knew the reason for any hesitancy; he just kept asking. Our relationship over the years wasn't always smooth, but I'll let him take credit.

IGNORANCE AND TERROR, GIFT AND GRACE

I've only lately been seeing a bigger picture in my little origin story, something true for us all: Before there's any "me" there's always a "we." Nobody comes into the world on their own. "The decision to begin living," as E. Lily Yu wrote, "is made for us." I am not myself by myself. Think you're self-made? Think again. Our existence happens blessedly before we are around, beyond anything we do. I didn't sign up. I didn't get a ballot to vote where I'd land. This coming into the world, Yu continued, is a passage "we embark upon in total ignorance and terror."[1] It's also a gift and grace. At every stage in my journey, people have formed me, sometimes disappointed me, and often loved me. A big *thanks*, most days at least, is so, *so* in order.

On an August Arizona morning, months after Kevin's plaintive, nagging "Please!" I joined the household. As I slipped from amniotic warmth, I faced the glaring shock of a brightly lit hospital room. I must have squinted, like any baby does—a lot. But my family welcomed me. I hope you can say something similar about your beginnings. And if you can't, well, more on that soon.

Now I picture my dad down the hall from the delivery room, with his clipped Massachusetts accent, saying, after hours in a Phoenix hospital waiting room full of pacing, cigarette-smoking dads: "Well, Kevin, you've got a brother now." Knowing his New England reserve, I doubt he said much more. Still, I envision him pleased to have another son.

With what I came to know of her stoic gentleness, I'd guess Mom would not have had much to say either, perhaps a grateful sigh or cooing sounds, as her arms held me—arms aching to embrace the human package of squirmy new life.

It wasn't a paradise in the mid-1950s—not for everybody at least—but I joined things at a more or less calm American moment, on a scrap of land cheerfully named the Valley of the Sun. I found life amid an arid desert that was turning into a bustling city. Residential yards of citrus and luminous green lawns hinted at the buzzing life.

It's no little thing to come into the world sensing you're wanted, finding, even as an infant, that the household you come home to makes room for you. (*Thank you, Lord.*) My brother was right in his version of my coming-into-the-world story: I owe others bigtime. A giant knitting project takes place, fingered needles looping around our strand of yarn and deftly weaving us in. "For you created my inmost being; you knit me together in my mother's womb," the psalmist prayed.[2] God makes us, in turn, part of something downright grand and sometimes puzzling. Whatever and wherever the placement, we owe others more than can be measured.

Maybe I'm not as coolly self-sufficient as I'd like to think some days. (A big temptation for our culture. More on that, too, later.) It's possible to die alone, as someone once said, but you cannot be born alone. You were *brought* in. Behind it all—behind anyone—things and people and choices come together. We get our start through the conspiring and affection (and sometimes the poor choices) of others. Larger forces and little human decisions worked overtime. It took a team effort: skill and prayer and mistakes. Some people may not have been sure what they were doing, but they still managed to stick our landing.

Our wider culture admires the so-called individualist, of course, the proud do-life-yourselfer. But we also sense the puffed-up preening feels a bit off. Some of us are rediscovering how much living is about relating, connecting, and recognizing what we owe to family or community. We are relational through and through. Our connecting ties to others are not mere threads; they are lifelines. "All true living is encounter," said the Jewish theologian Martin Buber.[3] A person is less an island and more an intersection. People can seem, I know, like bumper cars colliding at a state fair ride. But we belong *together.* We are made not by ourselves but in and through our interactions with others. We cannot thrive otherwise.

It's easy, though, isn't it, to fall into a comparison game? We pursue status when what we really want is belonging. Online media does not help this temptation. We measure our achievements—or our vacations—against the curated milestones of our internet world—sunshiny, beach-lit smiles of a family we know. Maybe I get FOFB—Fear of Falling Behind. This isn't about community; it's about thinking we can prove our worth or improve our standing. We compete, adding to a toxic climate frayed by division, much of it enflamed online. But in our attention-driven mediasphere, we are aching for more than online "likes." We want more, at least in our best moments. Something like real-time, flesh-and-blood relating.

Isn't the cry of your heart, the core desire at play, about more than your style or accessories or accomplishments? Doesn't it have to do with voices and faces and gentle gestures like a hand offered in invitation?

I was thinking about all this while watching my daughter carry her first child just months ago. Bekah and her husband turned their faces toward her belly and spoke to the life in her womb. They laughed as they told me about it. And if you are tempted to find that a tiny bit comical, know this: By the stirring response Bekah felt from the little life within, they were convinced that, even then, little Eva could recognize that someone was addressing her. Here were voices I'll wager she listened for. I love that thought. A kick from inside signaled the wonder of a person poking and elbowing her way into conscious existence, delighting in some primal way in a safe place to grow. Her parents knew a life was growing wildly, wonderfully within, and they wanted to ready her even then to find joy in the conversations that would later unfold.

How did our parents carry *us*? It could have been that way with you and me too. We begin as a gestating, curled-up question mark, waiting to be ushered—or pushed—into the answering open. We had a lot to take in. I can't imagine the kaleidoscope of sensations—except that I get a little hint when I watch Eva, now six months old, wide-eyed with curiosity, intently staring at the world around her—especially the faces.

Next time you see a baby, notice how they soak up everything and everyone around them, like a sponge, or like tiny explorers scanning new territory with every glance or sound. And while the glint of sunlight or a sudden movement of some object catches their attention, they especially watch for ways to connect. Aren't they on the lookout for more than a mild face, but a smile? Isn't there a longing stirring already that will eventually lead us to the One who made us?

FIRST TO FORM: THE HEART

From the earliest days, something beats deep in us. Is it any accident that the heart is the first organ to form? This muscle, more than any other throughout human history, stands as a sign of our relatedness, the star of every rom-com, sonnet, and anatomy textbook for, well, centuries. Make that millennia. The heart "is smaller than a comma when it begins," wrote Brian Doyle, "and ends up bigger than a fist. Every cell in it is capable of pulsing. No one knows how that could be."[4]

But maybe we do know—a little, anyway. Our heart beats to larger powerful rhythms like you hear at a stadium rock concert, but deeper, more profound. Life is pulsing, pounding all around. "Up above my head," goes the great gospel song, "I hear music in the air."[5]

And all of this helps us makes sense of a God who, in the Trinity, shows us relationship before time. Our makeup has elements of earth and stardust, human desires and fragile hopes, and nothing less than the divine at work. Here, the mysterious becomes something more like the miraculous. To the best of our human efforts—the earthiness of human love—comes an infusion of divine artistry. It all makes for a recipe of messy, blessed, beloved extravagance. Emphasis on *blessed*. And *beloved*.

MORE THAN A DISTANT FORCE

Since I've been pondering the Trinity, I've become more alert to how the heart of the universe is no solo, loveless, blind randomness. This is part of what I want to convey to you, dear reader—how the Trinity helps us. The divine here is not just a force to "be with you" like in the *Star Wars* movies. It's good to acknowledge, as those movies do, something "out there." But sometimes that recognition ends with little idea of what such a reality looks like, feels like.

But *don't* we have an idea? We do, when we recall what riches we've inherited in this ancient belief, which opens a picture of relational beauty. God meets us in supremely personal ways as not only a force and Creator and Maker but also as our Father. The shift from Creator to paternal, parental Maker makes a difference. At least it does for me, and for many others.

C. S. Lewis recalled, "A girl I knew was brought up by 'higher thinking' parents to regard God as a perfect 'substance'; in later life she realized that this had actually led her to think of Him as something like a vast tapioca pudding. (To make matters worse, she disliked tapioca.)"[6]

God meets us in supremely personal ways as not only a force and Creator and Maker but also as our Father.

I'll take Father, Son, and Holy Spirit over that picture any day. At the foundation of all things is a God abounding in eager relating. The picture you carry around of the originator of the universe affects your small, everyday choices. If God is stingy, mean-spirited, aren't we sunk? But if relating to the divine means not a mushy lack of boundaries but beings who relate in freedom and delighted conversation—if instead God is kind—will that not temper what we despair about?

But maybe it's not quite so rosy, you might think. I know I can look at my family of origin and see how they opened the lap of their household but also sometimes dropped their catches. There were improvised verbal weapons to step around, relational territory where I had to tread gingerly. "I wish," wrote Anne Lamott, "the movement of love in our lives more closely resembled the grace of a ballerina, but no, love mainly tromps and plops, falls over and tiptoes through our lives."[7] If you chuckle at that image, you have good reason.

And I know this now: To want to be loved and to want to love comes with costs. To care risks stumbling over the fickleness of human love. To stay connected opens us to the world's fragile aspects. The measure of our love leads to the weight of its loss. We run toward others, only to then ram into the prospect of being turned aside, even bruised.

No wonder I'm drawn to an old doctrine that keeps putting a God of familial love at the center of our conversations. I find language written with vivid characters—a story of Father and Son. Here is language the youngest child can use, names the child in the very adult *us* can call up. We think we have to "find God" through our spiritual "journey." But central and essential to life is a God who both makes us and seeks us—who goes looking for us and addresses us even when we rest in the womb. If our identity comes from what we're given, if divine grace is the starting place, then we see how God has kept us in eyeshot all along. The good news starts with God's initiative, not ours.

Central and essential to life is a God who both makes us and seeks us—who goes looking for us and addresses us even when we rest in the womb.

RUMMAGING IN THE STORIES OF A CHILD

Augustine, the North African bishop, rummaged through stories of his childhood in a way his contemporaries in the ancient world hadn't thought of. Or if they did, they looked down on trying to find clues there. Like him—and partly because of reading his work—I've started thinking more about how the people around me shaped me. I imagine you sometimes think about how your early years shaped who you are too.

Augustine's reflection helped him see a bigger story. He didn't believe he could understand his life from only the moment at hand, from only today's whims or hopes. Instead, to make sense of the enormous project living becomes, he looked back at both the good and painful moments, his current trials and his earliest aspirations. Augustine might have said with the psalmist, "From birth I was cast on you; from my mother's womb you have been my God."[8] I see him sifting through the precious memories and the harsh moments to see in it all a bigger picture.

And I see him discerning God right there, from the barest beginnings.

His searching got intense. Augustine churned out three hundred letters, five hundred sermons, dozens of commentaries, and some impressively fat books that could double as doorstops—all in pursuit of answers. Did the man ever find time to sleep? I imagine as a child he might have been allergic to naps.

And if you don't have the gumption to dip toes in this body of work, I can give some highlights. Perhaps the bishop is best known for his poignant account of his life and faith in his *Confessions*. There, he looked at the arc of his story, refusing to gloss over the tensions. And he was on the lookout for what happened that would both explain and fuel his longing for more. Even back then he could sense that he would never be complete, at least in this life. What could give the peace that both tantalized and eluded him? It's less a *what* and more like a big *who*. Here's where perhaps we can all feel connected to him: Who doesn't want to love and be loved? To relate more richly, not only as a creature of God but also as a child of God, even in the midst of our hardest, most hopeful, and most formative times?

And he helps me when I see the unflinching way he explored what he actually lived through. I wonder what you have found in those times you reflect on the unfolding encounters of your life.

Maybe you have trouble putting some of the painful ones to rest. They keep you from sound sleep. Maybe then, sensing the possibility you, too, might understand, you take comfort from Augustine's story.

There's something down to earth, so to speak, about someone who wants to sift through the normal conversations and disappointments that made him who he was. He knew these things made him long for God, made him hope. He wrote on the off chance that his readers would come across something they might recognize in themselves—a glimpse of what can be. So he kept writing and telling.

He knew the longing for God traces back. Way back. It did for me.

SHOT THROUGH WITH CONNECTION

A bit older, I wore striped short-sleeved T-shirts and faded dusty jeans, just right for the joys of California and Arizona mornings. I'd run in the SoCal sunshine and among the trees in our Phoenix yards, bursting with lemons and oranges. I played "cowboys and Indians" with my neighbor friends, oblivious to the heartache and bloodshed in that American backstory. No wonder that, as I grew, I felt part of something. I loved this life to which I'd gotten a personal invitation.

My brother liked having a sibling. And when I came in from playing, I knew a caring adult would be around. However often we moved while I grew up, I found security—a table around which we gathered, always, sometimes just in a kitchen nook—a place where I belonged. People with whom I could have conversations that valued me.

So much so that when love seemed to ghost me, when my parents tried to squash my spirit and push me away, something in my heart mutinied. It didn't seem just in the deepest ways because of the bedrock of love I had known earlier; it came from the sense that love is bigger than that.

From the time I was a child—going without protest (if sometimes grudgingly) to Sunday school classes at my suburban Methodist churches—I heard the biblical belief about the world's creation by a vast God. "In the beginning *God*," the ancient account begins. In the beginning *God created* the heavens and the earth. This God ushered the world into reality. Even ushered *me.*

Creation seems shot through with *inter*connections, just as Rowan talked about when we chatted in his study. I've thought of simple and striking ways this works. Like oceans and their intricate watery ecosystems. And on dry land, there's a whole support network in the plant world—a leafy LinkedIn. Old wisdom held that trees competed for light, water, and minerals in the soil—but we now know they communicate through roots and billions of fungal cell filigree that grow from and connect with other trees. A lacelike linkage—a *network.* We can't see their underground communication system, but trees can send SOS signals, check in with withering siblings, or even transfer tide-you-over nutrients to neighbors when things get rough and dry. And that's just *trees.* Trying to trace other interrelated processes across the vast earth could make your head spin.

And all the more with us—human beings, the pinnacle of creation. I try to stay alert to how much of the relationality Rowan described intertwines with everything we do or attempt. Birth itself seems like a miracle of coordination. I think of the interweaving of lives in a family that works, or a small group of friends that click and then nurture one another. Consider cities. Neighborhoods. Churches. Even the disaster of fracturing politics and community conflict points to what *could* be—glimmers that point back to an original vision from God. A picture of what the Bible calls shalom—heavenly harmony made earthly.

NO MERE LUCK OR IFFY COINCIDENCE

No wonder the idea of God as relational, what the old poet and priest John Donne called "the three-person'd God," resonates. Relationality, worked and kneaded into reality through and through, cannot help but shine out.

In Scripture, we get a timeline going way further back, preceding us by eons, of an everlasting being at home with relating. Our connecting has a cosmic backdrop—a Divinity for whom interaction is a natural, a given. When you have a God who is one in three, already in relationship before creating the world, you can expect relationship to exist at the core. For we see a creativity that has a relational feel, not simply a mechanical or aesthetic "big bang."

Such linking provides a partial mirror to other life at work, not only in sociology or biology but also in how God moves. For there's more going on with my being made than I first thought. Not just Kevin's persistent pitch to Mom and Dad that they grant him the gift of a sibling. I mean how the Trinity compounds our comprehension of things. Take a scrap of a psalm: "You created my inmost being."[9] *You created me,* made me, the psalmist said to God—reassuring us that the universe has at its foundation not dumb luck or iffy coincidence but purposeful reality.

Creation, then, is more than an artful assemblage. God uses the material he made all around us and fashions from it something especially magnificent: a person. He's willing to rework this masterpiece, too, as any patient artist could and would.

For this is no vaguely disinterested deity at work, off working in solitary reveries. And as God fashioned the world—creating something out of nothing, as the first book of the Bible tells us—it was more than lonesome work. There's delighted collaboration. For centuries scholars have puzzled over the moment when God said, "Let *us* make humankind." Make people in *our* image. But I see a hint here.

Not a proof of the Trinity but a glimmer. Yes, *God* created, not gods, Scripture tells us. One God. Yet the Trinity matters here—hugely. For from before time began, there was confraternity. A community. Boggling the mind, eternity past brims with relationship.

More hints and clues pointing to the richness: We see how *wind*, often translated as "spirit" or "breath," moved over the face of the unformed waters. This high-flying entity is not something flighty. Even in these primordial beginnings, the Spirit didn't just move or hang or hover; it brooded—in the best possible way, as in solicitous care. Think of a bird minding its eggs or hatchlings. God through the Spirit is "above the face" of the water.

Here is not some airy (or agitated) vagueness. Order and beauty grow out of the Spirit's active participation. A celestial conversation does more than shoot the breeze. God's interrelatedness does more than settle for the superficial. It moves worlds—and human persons—into place with wind and breath. We witness a kind of divine choreography, stirring in us a renewed sense of a divinely guided creativity.

And God's "word," God's speaking, also had a hand in calling forth the world. Early Christians, reflecting on this mystery, came to recognize Jesus' role in this capital-*W* Word. If you think an artist can fashion something wonderful out of marble or clay or oil paints, consider all the more Jesus. Vincent van Gogh, pained though he was by despair at times in his life, saw Jesus as a supreme artist. And Jesus, in his cocreating role, shared in making something better than mountain peaks or statues or wall adornments. He made living people.

So there's more to it all—to *us*—than maybe we thought. Creation flowed out of a collegial interplay, directly enlisting the Spirit's breath, and Jesus, the Word, the movements of the divine intermingling. God shares such life and joy with us by making us, drawing us into the delight God already enjoys in eternal, triune love. "Christ plays in ten thousand places," said the poet, and I can begin to picture the sheer delighted, nimble joy.[10] God delighted in the making and working and speaking. What a lovely thought, that amid all the intensity and intentionality there was also play. There was lightness and generosity behind it.

Good words to counteract our perceived stuffiness of belief in God as Trinity! Our underlived hopes for what life can mean, the desperation we can feel, come face-to-face with something to lighten the heart.

God delighted in the making and working and speaking. What a delightful thought, that amid all the intensity and intentionality there was also play.

ARE WE EVER ALONE?

And there is more than play and artistry in the world God cherishes. There are also other clues to our belovedness. We see a God, more complex than we might have thought, who lives in sublime communion, who fathoms both the unseen molecules and the starry expanses, yet appears as close as our breath, as the oxygen that fills our newborn-to-this-world lungs or the hospital-issued blanket that clothes our little souls. We are still our separate selves, healthy and whole, but we are also our fullest characters only when we let people into our hearts. And then we let them point us to a higher intimacy. We consider how even in our little motions and small moments there lives and breathes a larger communion.

And we can know something about a larger world by extension. "My thoughts are not your thoughts . . . so are my ways higher than your ways," says the Lord.[11] Yes, we need to acknowledge that mysteriousness every morning as we get cranking for a day ahead. But we still take clues from what we see, the inherent interconnectedness. I ask more often, now that I'm pondering the Trinity—I ask more *urgently* a question I invite you to ask also: *In what ways do we stand in relation to a Being to whom we owe our very being?* Won't this allow us to better claim a promise that the universe is not cold, not spiraling into random aloneness, but rich with relational depths? Might we all feel a little less alone if we let that truth wash over us?

YOU DIDN'T JUST HAPPEN TO HAPPEN

It's easy enough to forget this dependence on God—our "madeness." In our rush to curate our identities we may lose sight of that. And what we manage to acquire and possess has less to do with who we are than we might think. We are not, fundamentally, our "stuff." Still, if we just try harder, accumulate enough, impress more, won't life seem richer, finally full?

It won't. Not if, as Scripture stresses, we don't just "happen," but we are instead wonderfully made, as the psalmist put it, by a God whose triunity hints at riches we may overlook. Our belovedness grows from deeper roots. Augustine quoted Psalm 139 more than once: "On you I was cast from my birth and since my mother bore me you have been my God."[12] There is no truly solitary self because we always stand interconnected with others. And in the biggest way: I've been given a start by a conspiring community of creativity in the Trinity.

We get hints every day that life is infused with Presence. "Where can a living being such as an infant come from," asked Saint Augustine, "if not from you, God? Or can anyone become the cause of his own making?"[13] We are dependence through and through. The world is *inter*dependence through and through. This means we owe divine Providence big-time.

There is no truly solitary self because we always stand interconnected with others. And in the biggest way: I've been given a start by a conspiring community of creativity in the Trinity.

MORE THAN MONEY MANAGEMENT

My own efforts at self-determination make me aware of how little I can manipulate. "Take control of your financial future," an ad promises. Remake your personality, is the summons, through some life hacks and simple steps. But any efforts at reinventing myself will bump into some perimeter walls and smack into some givens.

A positive outlook has its place but so does facing honest limits. The slogan "You can become whatever you want to be" is a bald-faced untruth, fit only for alternate worlds I've yet to discover, not even when I watch *Star Trek* reruns. What we *want* alone does not always determine our trajectory or destiny. You can't simply yearn to be an astronaut or professor or prodigy and find it become reality. Same with willing yourself to prosperity. Limits matter. I have parts of my personality, for instance, that make me who I am and, I can see, some people find precious. But also annoying habits of relating and ingrained patterns that can hurt another. Why do I leave doors and cabinets half-open, as if someone else will come along and finish the job?

Even if I wanted to, could I make a life without sometimes messing up? More on this reality in a later chapter, but for now, while it means admitting my limits, it also means a bit of release from the pressure of an incessant personal growth bucket list. I'd like a little let-up, personally.

There's something humbling and oddly comforting here. A bit funny too. And freeing. To know we are not the ultimate authors of our lives gives us a break. Isn't there a surprising freedom in *not* being God full time—or even a part-time assistant? Who truly wants all that responsibility? And mapping out my whole life, much less another's? No thanks. I can barely keep up with my everyday life's to-do list.

So much for the current trend of thinking we can tailor

everything to our preferences. That we can "manifest" the things we dream about and are jonesing for. I don't see how, as one overly optimistic, over-caffeinated self-help book subtitle suggested, I can create my life from the inside out. We don't quite have that authority or autonomy, even in the name of spirituality.

If we start with our belovedness, we see something clearer about our identities: We are not our job titles, bank accounts, or the random accomplishments we throw on a résumé to sound like we've got everything in hand, right on schedule, thanks very much. What we need is not brazen self-confidence, but a chastened openness. My chance to live and flourish was not wrested but gifted. If we all come from some place, and some *Ones*, we also owe life to a Someone. If our making grew out of a divine community then we have a connection that overarches us and grounds us. It's not self-invention we need but self-offering. Willing participation with what the triune God started—a long time ago. Delighting in our being made—the freedom and possibilities.

I still get weighed down some days by the achievement-oriented household that oohed and ahhed at recognition and awards and accomplishments. I'm not sorry I got my Eagle Scout award from Boy Scouts. I learned good skills and made new friends as I earned what they called merit badges. I am grateful I learned the difference between a square knot and a granny knot. Out in the woods, I can spot poison ivy in a flash. But I also felt what I did sometimes as a pressure. Almost as a compulsion to prove my worth—*merit* proved by *badges*.

LOOSEN UP, WAG MORE

In glimmers of the Trinity's interconnectedness, we see possibilities of needed freedom from thinking it's all up to us. Maybe we can loosen up a bit, lighten up a lot. "Wag more, bark less," as one bumper sticker says. *Obsess* less, maybe.

I was moved the first time my brother, Kevin, told me about his role in my coming onto the planet. I still am. *Thank you, Kevin,* for asking our folks to, well, make *me* possible. And the larger, transcendent debt still moves me: It's not our earning or scheming. God did not—and does not—*need* us. In ways I see more clearly now than ever, God is warmly and forever happy to be God. But God's love overflows and chooses to create. It's all about a divine enduing, his gifting. We are pre-owned. Pre-*loved.*

Out of that brimming ocean of swirling life and universe of unceasing movement, God makes us with the expectation that his love will be enough, whatever we face.

NOT TO BE GLIB, BUT . . .

But maybe the world is scarier than that.

Can spiritual assurances guarantee the world won't be a flaming dumpster some days, some places? That every wanted baby conceived will make it? I don't think so.

A renowned philosopher spoke of our human "thrownness."[14] I'm not fond of that image, the stomach-churning sensation of a carnival ride where I hurtle in a metal pod. But I know what he meant. We not only come into a world we didn't make, we also get tossed into a constellation of people we did not choose. They hold our flourishing in their grasp even while they sometimes knock a child's innocence off kilter, mess up the trajectory.

But the "thrownness" has another angle in light of the Trinity. When I was very small, my dad sometimes ventured out of the house to the yard where Kevin and I played. Dad didn't laugh much around our suburban house—he worked long hours in an office-lab as an aerospace engineer—but he smiled during those times under the California sun. He might toss me into the air, a foot or two or three. *A small sensation of thrownness.* I was tied to the earth but also, for a split moment, lofted above it.

I felt the thrill of being launched, but of his catching me too. For a breath-holding moment I hung above, suspended between earth and sky, my heart fluttering a bit, but always I landed in firm, expansive hands. For it feels like we are not tossed but rather *placed* into a constellation of people who make us and shape us.

Sarah Condon, a friend of mine, was asked when her son was born, "How are you going to tell him about how hard the world can be?" She replied, "The world will do enough of that on its own. My job is to care for him and love him." That picture rings true: People love us into resilience against the onslaughts, the slings and arrows.

So yes, where we land holds risks. We might be showered with fiercely stubborn love. I wish everyone were. But sometimes conception itself involves violation and violence, and birth involves cruelty or neglect. I hope it wasn't so for you. A child may be abused, scalded, raped. I think of babies born amid all the bloodshed of Ukraine's war. They soon realize, in their earliest inklings, what kind of place they've landed in.

What do we do when we hear reports of a boarding school for the visually impaired bombed, a bus carrying orphaned children out of danger blocked, families huddled in subways for weeks, weeping couples separating at the border? All this *before* the horrific suffering in Gaza and Israel, with schools and homes left in rubble. What spiritual response makes sense when we see tear-streaked, defiant, afraid faces? When our screens and devices deliver constant news of the miseries and horrors of war?

Lord, have mercy.

For if what the Trinity says about our creation—our being made amid glorious conversations in the divine realms—holds, my friend

Sarah's son can know how special he is. Not just because of his mom and dad's remarkable love, but also in a larger way, a backdrop with cosmic proportions.

A DRASTIC REALITY BATHED IN MERCY

And maybe birth itself is a teeny bit more demanding than we realize. Pediatricians will tell you how jolting that passage is, how no time in life, not even our deaths, compares in intensity with the changes that happen.

We enter life amid a kind of blessed physical trauma. In an instant, for example, a newborn will take its first breath, its cry signaling that oxygen is filling lungs that never before held air. Someone snips a connecting cord, cutting off nutrients. Cupped hands must have reached out to catch me. I don't think they missed the pass. And you also hope a newborn gets skin-to-skin contact right away. That a new bonding happens.

For I opened my tender and swollen eyes that sweltering Phoenix morning at 8:39, needing to come to terms with a world I knew nothing about. I met the shock of a bright-lit entry, joining a new world outside the warm amniotic universe.

And I was, so to speak, all eyes. Once emerged, before long an infant enters a stage called "quiet alert." The young irises can focus within a range of only a foot or so, but still they scan for a face. They search for a set of eyes: *Where's Mom? Where's some kind face?*

What better conveys our relational bent? I lapse into such moments now, when I'm not too rushed, when I look lovingly and longingly at the faces of people in my life, I can begin, just possibly, to imagine how I would have then too. And when newborn eyes meet another's, especially eyes that return the gaze, they rivet *their* eyes to that face. They relate. They connect.

And right there, in language of Father, Son, and Holy Spirit that some have given up on, we catch glimmers of all this writ larger. We start with fundamental experiences of family—the places of our birth and formation, the giving of a mother's milk, a father holding us like a little football, our origin stories, just as wise Augustine reflected. And then, what if, as my friend Kathy said to me once, in the unfolding discoveries the church made about the Trinity, "Here is a story that takes seriously every category of human experience"? That blessed thought includes our barest, most fundamental beginnings.

We remember that we were made with care and love—especially important in a world that so often tries to strip away our humanity, ignore our feelings, or reduce us to nothing more than consumer data on a spreadsheet.

Ah, but if God fundamentally and unconditionally loves us and made a world out of love and for the purpose of love, then everything becomes more endurable, imbued with hints of meaning. It's less lonely. Here is a living God—loving, not distant or stand-offish.

CATCHING UP WITH MYSTERY

A woman I heard about tried an experiment. She had already decided she wanted to speak less in prayer and listen more, stay attuned to a larger voice. She sat in a chair and tried to imagine the Father, the Son, and the Holy Spirit in the room sitting around her, conversing and communing. "I wanted," she said, "to eavesdrop on the Trinity."

That approach took some imagination, but I admire her willingness to try. Some

We were made with care and love—especially important in a world that so often tries to strip away our humanity, ignore our feelings, or reduce us to nothing more than consumer data on a spreadsheet.

theologians get a little nervous talking too much about what this intra-Trinity community is like—there are mysteries here, and the inadequacy of human language strains. A whole stream of thought, called apophatic, stresses what we cannot say about God. The limits of language.

And we can be honest here, can't we? We love a God we know who is invisible and at times hard to read. Human categories can never explain a God who eludes by sheer glory our talky attempts. Admitting this gives us permission not to always have the words—not to *have to* have the words.

Some of us scratch our skeptical heads. What analogies from human life could possibly even come close to framing God's wonders? But if this is mystery, it is mystery personified. We get hints. A revelation. A hefty starting place. Rowan Williams said to me, when I interviewed him for a magazine, "Something has happened, which is the revelation of the Trinity, and we're all trying to catch up with it."[15]

I like that image. Not that he or I can promise that, in this life at least, we will fully grasp it. As much as a relational God warms our view of the divine, the reality will always outstrip our strides forward. We can say as clearly and accurately as we know and ask God for mercy for what we don't—or can't—know. But what of all that we *can* see and understand? It's worth pursuing.

IMAGINING BEYOND THE MATH

As we try to grow in our understanding of the Trinity, much of the talk I hear in the church trips us up on the arithmetic. Ireland's St. Patrick supposedly tried to make the mystery clear to his Irish listeners with a three-leaf clover: three leaf lobes, one stem. Three Persons, one God. Or water: It comes in three forms—liquid, steam, ice, yet in all the variation, still H_2O.

But do little mental gimmicks like that really help? Living with an awareness of three Persons within God tells us that we can expect more than object lessons.

Especially helpful, I find, is to notice our own interconnections, the communal realities at work in human life, birth, and relating. These offer a taste of what God offers, better than mere intellectual insight. I've just learned that the Hebrew word for mercy comes from the same root as *womb*. And here we see again great graces in how we begin life. There, in our dark, enclosed origins, we form and grow. Only then do we join the outside world, and perhaps there find mercy as well, continuing to grow in who we are and in whose we can become.

HOW YOU WRITE YOUR *I*

One day I was in the back seat of the family car as we went on some errand to a store. Kevin, up front, was talking about something he had heard regarding how handwriting reveals your personal makeup. If you make your capital *I* with a vertical dash and two horizontal strokes top and bottom, he said, it shows self-confidence. Not with loopy cursive curves, in other words. I had no idea if there was any truth to that interpretation and whether handwriting really tells others about our personality traits. Some say handwriting analysis is shaky science, unfounded. But I liked the idea of what Kevin said.

"I do that!" I said. No one up front responded—not out of rudeness, just silence.

"I write my *I* like that," I said again, trying to show who I was, proud of this little detail. Like saying, "Yes, I make my *I*'s like someone who knows things."

But that small, hopeful pride would soon be shaken. Something would come that challenged who I was becoming—tested the new feeling of being seen and loved. A blow that would take a while to gain force, emerge only when I came of age, when I was finally bold to make my own irreversible decisions. The need for affirmation would be tested.

Thank God for a backdrop, for glimmers I glimpsed early on, an expansive picture that would keep me from getting discouraged over what was to come.

THREE

HOW WILL LOVE FIND ME IN THE BREATHTAKING AND THE HEARTBREAKING?

The world is charged with the grandeur of God.
It will flame out, like shining from shook foil.
—Gerard Manley Hopkins

And what is the object of my love? I asked the earth and it said: "It is not I." I asked all that is in it; they made the same confession. . . . I asked heaven, sun, moon and stars; they said: "Nor are we the God whom you seek." . . . And with a great voice they cried out: "He made us."
—Saint Augustine

As a mother comforts her child [says the Lord],
so will I comfort you.
—Isaiah 66:12–13

HAVE YOU EVER TAKEN A TRIP THAT HELD AN UNEXpected encounter? I thought it would be a mundane excursion one Saturday.

That morning my mom, my dad, Kevin, and I piled into our Chevrolet station wagon. We left behind the cars and smog—the stale emissions and haze hanging over our suburb. We drove toward a semirural setting a couple of hours out, hoping for some quiet, some escape.

I don't remember everything we did during our one-day outing—a stop at a California town with quaint bakeries, maybe a fudge shop with sugary smells, a place to get a burger. On the return trip home, I stretched out in the back compartment. This was before you had to wear seat belts, and the rear of a wagon could be your personal nap space. I could see, through the sloping back window, the night sky. Not just any glimpse, though. The glow of city lights had always dimmed the stars back home, turning the sky into a giant gray napkin with flecks of dulled glitter.

But now, in a canopy washed clean of pollutants, I saw the Milky Way. In the dark backcountry, I could see the stars spattered in a vivid, twinkling band. Pinpoints to my eyes but also scintillating specks of light—a glimpse of a lit hugeness above. Who knew that a day beginning with a weekend excursion would thrust me into the presence of heavenly altitudes?

I didn't have the words then to understand everything I was sensing. I might have pointed and said something to Kevin, probably dozing in the bench seat in front of me. But I held the experience close, kept it to myself. The majestic beauty I witnessed would have been hard to put into words anyway.

Any child experiences the world as big, with things happening above, having always to tilt a head when around the adults towering above. Maybe you remember looking up to the big people in your life. Maybe you looked up in other ways—at treetops, skyscraper heights, or mountains. But in this glimpse, in a scene so panoramic, the effect so dramatic, I see it as one of my first awarenesses of God. You might call it awe at first sight. I don't know if what stirred in me was exactly praise and prayer, but I felt an awakening to wonder. I stretched out under a shimmering quiet radiance. It seemed more impressive than anything I'd seen.

I think the vast sky opened a sensitivity in me I hadn't had before. There was an abundance here, even in the range of sight of a child. It felt like the universe was showing off, giving a kind of cosmic light show.

WHAT THE HEAVENS DECLARE

Humankind has looked up and almost universally concluded that belief in a benevolent beginning to the world explains a lot of what we see and sense. It's the "intuition found widely in ancient religion," wrote Marilynne Robinson, "that the universe did indeed have a beginning."[1] Again and again, we conclude that there are more than random assortments of atoms in play. "When I look at your heavens, the work of your fingers, the moon and the stars which you set in place—what is a human being that you think of him? And a child of humankind that you care for him?"[2]

Even a child can stop in awe before a sky full of beauty and lit-up glory. "Since the creation of the world," wrote the apostle Paul, "God's invisible qualities—his eternal power and divine nature—have been clearly seen, being understood from what has been made."[3] How many times have you heard someone say, "I don't see how this universe could have just *happened*"?

And how many times have you been brought up short by the realization of a "something more" permeating the world? The purely physical leaves vapor trails of the cosmic. The microscopic opens to a teeming world of tiny glories. A forest of trees contains amazing intricacies. Sometimes snow washes the city air and freshens the earth, making it all seem even clearer, cleaner, imbued with divine goodness.

My friend Louise was sledding one winter night with her boys, and she saw something quiet and hard to express that had to do with all this. In the middle of the running and laughing, she told me, she took a moment to lay down in the snow, cold though it was, and look up at the night sky. They all did. Moments like that, she said, "leave me amazed and in awe of God." We fumble for words to express what we encounter. But we can feel it effervescing inside us when we hear a phrase like, "The heavens declare the glory of God," as the psalm says.[4] Do Louise's boys, all these years later, recall that night?

And it's not just the orange-pink glories of dawn, not just a constellated sky, not just the majesty of rocky peaks; it's also the vividness and vibrancy of all kinds of life—the impossibly tiny leaves of moss. Soon, on camping trips with the Boy Scouts, I became enamored with the maples and aspens, the dragonflies and praying mantises. On a coastal vacation, the Oregon tidepools amazed me with the finger-like, ticklish tentacles of sea anemones. The comedy of skittering hermit crabs. The glory of a cottontail deer, startled by human approach, bounding away. The litter of mewling kittens born—to our surprise—in our basement early in our marriage. Or the life of a hummingbird: "Each one visits a thousand flowers a day. They can dive at sixty miles an hour. They can fly backwards." Their "race-car hearts" beat ten times a second.[5] And most miraculous of all: a baby born squalling, eyes flooded with light, as ours were—miracle of miracle—from the attraction and interaction of two people.

Sometimes a dimension, there all along, emerges in clear view, right where we are. I must have caught hints of that realm before that night under the Milky Way. I certainly experienced something warming and enlarging before then, just being cocooned in the warmth of hearth, car trips, and splashing in a neighborhood pool. But this time was different. More visceral and real. More doused in awe.

My friend David Bannon found this while walking near his home. "Our world is awash with suffering," he admitted, thinking of his own grief at losing his daughter to an overdose. But, he wrote, "it is also redolent of meaning, aroma, and unexpected joys. Hiking for hours and miles in the deep wood surrounding our home, I am frequently stunned by what I missed before. The tiniest flower or tallest conifer is a source of peace. Once I may have tromped past, overlooking their delicate, fleeting fragrance. Now I seek them out. Have you ever noticed the smell of trees?"[6]

We can forget all this or ignore our hunger with the help of distractions and diversions. Augustine wrote profoundly about what happened when he averted his focus from God. He admitted to God the futility of finding a resting place apart from a vital relationship with God: "The soul rolls back and forth onto its back, onto one side and then another, onto its stomach, but every surface is hard, and you're the only rest."[7] He meant *his* soul. I think of ours. Don't we all carry what someone called an ache for cosmic specialness? A yearning for a divine Someone, kind and close by?

Some days I forget that we live in a Presence-saturated universe, as I was beginning to discover as a child. Maybe it's because of how I've grown used to the quick, superficial scan. I turn away quickly instead of turning a lingering look to our world or to others. "There's a cosmic energy about God's Creation," wrote poet Paul Mariani, "an electrical charge, both violent and violet sweet, ready to instress itself upon us if only we will pay it the attention it deserves."[8]

WORDS EVEN A CHILD CAN GRASP

All the glory points to a stunning start—to intentionality and artistry. In some ways, it's simple. For many, perhaps for you, God the Creator first caught your awe and attention.

The early biblical creation accounts, for all their majesty, appeared with unfussy concreteness. As recorded in Genesis, God spoke the world into existence using words so concrete that everyone could picture the work: day, night, trees, birds, fish—words that could be captured in a child's picture book.

What I saw as a child planted seeds of holy suspicion that the universe, whatever else it was or wasn't, shone with the mystery of something *more.* That darkness, even with the pinholes of light, wasn't and couldn't be all.

I don't know why I was so struck at that moment. Or why I was then and some still aren't. But what I saw deepened a sense that what stretched out above me took some serious *making.* There had to be a hand in the handiwork. A child sees a parent *making* something—kneading yeasty bread, shaping the legs of a chair in a workshop, creating music on a keyboard, or, with my dad, fashioning jewelry from turquoise and silver—and gets a clue about a larger person fashioning what comes about. For those of us with an impulse to create—a sculpture, song, sonnet—we see encouragement to continue. "God created," wrote Makoto Fujimura, "because it is in God's nature to make and create. . . . God created out of abundance and exuberance, and the universe (and we) exist because God loves to create."[9]

When I look back, I wonder: When I heard the idea of a Maker of heaven and earth in the creeds we would say in Sunday church, did I feel a connection to a larger *something* because of what I saw in that nighttime sky in the back seat? I imagine I began to ask deeper questions.

Questions like, Was there a guiding God behind creation's creative spectacles? In the first few verses of the Bible, when we read of God's creating, we learn that "the earth was formless and empty, darkness was over the surface of the deep, and the Spirit of God was hovering over the waters."[10] Or, in another version, the earth was complete chaos. I would have heard the verses in Sunday school and learned that out of that murky soup came something ordered, intended—not haphazard. Was I beginning to sense how God is above creation, vastly so, but still connected to it? I could easily have tied the security I felt at home to the assurance I was beginning to feel from nature's glories.

I had my own anxieties, as any child will, but here I could imagine more at work. Anyone's life is "a brief crack of light between two eternities of darkness," wrote Vladimir Nabokov. "The cradle rocks above an abyss."[11] Sheesh, that's bleak. He didn't see much reassurance from the heavenlies. He didn't pay much attention, it seems, to glimmerings of glory in ways that led him to ask deeper questions.

But I was already getting hints that the universe is not an abyss yawning under a cradle. Not with what happens next in the creation account. For both renderings—*formless and empty* or *complete chaos*—picture utter incompleteness. The night of nothingness required more than ordering or organizing; it took an infusion. A massive construction from scratch but also a Being who could impart something as mysterious and enchanting as life. Doesn't such a drift of reasoning begin to set the stage for a fuller sense of belovedness? It's a start.

And something happens in the creation accounts I'm only now noticing. You could make a case that at the beginning of the world, when God speaks, "Let there be . . ." it is *light* that appears as the first created thing. Light served to illumine our lives and keep us from the worrying dark. Sun and stars—yes, they would come. Land and water, plants and animals—yes. But the showing forth of light itself had to happen first. It had to be *made.*

And it was night-sky light that so impressed itself on me. Light to establish sight in the dark skies and steal from them their power to evoke incessant fear. More than the solidity of objects, it was also the shining of suns. In his universe-making, God starts with matter, then moves on to flinging bright into the inky night.

At the beginning of the world, when God speaks, "Let there be . . ." it is light that appears as the first created thing. Light served to illumine our lives and keep us from the worrying dark.

The ancients knew that light would rescue us when we glimpse the dawn after a restless dark night with bad dreams. Light also makes you alert, flashing a warning. Illumination guides, the way an oil lamp or a light switch in a dark room leaves your eyes adjusting for a moment, but at least you don't bark your shins on furniture as you walk to the kitchen for water. In a universe that can look grim, knowing this makes all the difference. Seemingly impenetrable darkness becomes a backdrop for miraculous illumination. How thoughtful of God!

Not that I saw all this that night. But I would eventually. I'd see how moments of the breathtaking—and heartbreaking, for that matter—point beyond themselves. Sometimes a glance out the car window catches the eye. Later, when Jill and I fell for each other, I learned how a loved one's face bathed in the flickering light from a fireplace can reorient me. Even glimpses stolen from a hectic day put me back in touch. Reconnect me. I try to sit still, knowing, as Flannery O'Connor said, that sunlight can make the meanest (commonest) tree shine in radiant glory.[12]

The glory can amaze too. I place Nabokov's dreary portrait next to Annie Dillard's paean to the Maker: "The creator goes off on one wild, specific tangent after another, or millions simultaneously, with an exuberance that would seem to be unwarranted, and with an abandoned energy sprung from an unfathomable font."[13] There's joy here. God delights in not only the world's wonders but also in its sons and daughters.

Once God asked Job—the poor man hurting, tired, unable to imagine much beyond his own grief and daily grind—

Can you bind the chains of the Pleiades?
Can you loosen Orion's belt?
Can you bring forth the constellations in their seasons
or lead out the Bear with its cubs?
Do you know the laws of the heavens?
Can you set up God's dominion over the earth?[14]

They were rhetorical questions, of course, pointedly asked. But they eventually helped lift Job out of his distress. When I saw Pleiades or Orion, not knowing what to call them, that station wagon glimpse taught me to look outward, heavenward, and to ponder mysteries I might have thought I had no reason to consider.

Later, too, I heard about the delight Francis of Assisi found in nature and how the created universe stirred in him a hum of ecstatic astonishment. He wrote *The Canticle of Brother Sun*, proclaiming,

Praised be You, my Lord, through Sister Moon and the stars,
in heaven you formed them clear and precious and beautiful.[15]

I think that's what began to awaken in me that night on a California backroad: a sense that some sights point to a glory beyond the routine of churchgoing in my family. A world formed as not only beautiful but also precious.

I could snatch a glance at One who could make himself seen and known. God so loved the world, you could say, that he made himself glimpsable. As I could now see, in creation we get more than an intuition but also a revelation: The world spins around an intention to create, a will to plant beauty, and a desire, ultimately, to love.

The world spins around an intention to create, a will to plant beauty, and a desire, ultimately, to love.

Might I have been primed that night to think of existences above and beyond my reach yet eager to bid my attention? C. S. Lewis spoke of a secret desire we have, a yearning for another realm that this little world cannot completely satisfy. Lewis used the idea of *sehnsucht*, a German word meaning longing desire, an aching pleasantness and nostalgia for what was and can be. It may embarrass us sometimes with its seeming strangeness, but it also pierces us with its sweetness. And the longing it stirs in us points us to another realm, another place.

GOD MADE PERSONAL

Here is where things get more personal. Awe rises within us, but so does something deeper, more intimate. The Bible stresses all kinds of things about God through word pictures: a stone wall's strength, a tree, cooling water, an eagle's wings. Even the seemingly impersonal images have relational aspects, though—for instance, God as a Rock of refuge, a burning bush that captures Moses' attention, living water that purifies and restores the soul, or eagles' wings on which God says "I bore you."[16] Imagery such as husband-wife, parent-child, or teacher-learner carries even more personal meaning. Consider the stone-of-strength variation in Deuteronomy, where God spoke through Moses and said, "You deserted the Rock, who fathered you; you forgot the God who gave you birth."[17] Both maternal and paternal—both highly personal.

"It seems to me," wrote theologian Michael Lloyd, "that as human beings, we warm to . . . know that it is a Person who is behind reality and responsible for it."[18] A God who will not go absent from the creatures in whom he tenderly breathed life. Who, in the words of fourteenth-century mystic Julian of Norwich, shows himself maker, lover, and keeper of all that is. Who tends the world—and our world—fully and dramatically.

For God not only flung expanses of beauty across a night sky; he also became, for me, as the biblical story unfolds—as my story unfolds—like a heavenly Father. Here lies a balm to what my friend once called cosmic orphanhood. Julie Canlis captured this conviction well: "Written into the heart of the universe . . . is open and free conversation between us and God; [a certainty] that the universe is *personal*; that time rushes over a bedrock of love."[19]

I look back on my earliest sightings and realize how they would grow into a wider vision. They primed me to see, later, that Being has more depth and interrelatedness than we may first realize. That God cared enough to make not automatons, but humans who could relate to him. Can you look back and notice the first sparks of such insight in your own life—perhaps even in early life? In those small glimpses of wonder, you may have been more of a child theologian than you knew.

"If you were growing up pagan in ancient Mesopotamia," wrote pastor Matt Canlis, your parents would help you make sense of the world and the tribal gods through stories. And that story said humans came into the world because the gods needed slaves. "This was the preferred bedtime story Pharaoh hoped his slaves would use to tuck in their children. It would reinforce their demeaned place in society." But the Bible took another tack. "Hebrew parents told a different story. . . . God didn't need slaves. God wanted children."[20] When the Genesis account appeared in writing, after ages of oral transmission, there was something warmly personal about it.

Here is a God fashioning human beings—persons "wonderfully made," as the psalm I would learn put it. Personally made. A world made out of kindness. As Rowan Williams suggested to me in his study, relationship, a personal quality, was embedded in it all from the world's start.

MORE THAN CREATED, DEEPLY CARED FOR

An illustrated book saved from childhood has accompanied me through well more than a dozen moves and surely fed my awakening to the world's wonders. My brother, in a child's hand, scribbled his name on the inside front cover, so it's clearly a hand-me-down. But the book became mine, in more ways than one. Perhaps a book or story or illustration from your childhood affects you even now and lives on in its impact.

All these decades later, something in me grows still when I open the frayed edges of the cardboard covers. *Prayers for Children* now strikes me especially for the visuals—famed artist Eloise Wilkin's cherub-cheeked children with a dreamy, soft focus to the colored pencil and watercolor scenes of rural calm and home-like loveliness. I notice now a closing spread with a lit-up night sky.

Earlier in the pages, the prayer I notice is titled "Dear Father, Hear and Bless."

Intertwined with the stanza, a tousle-headed boy holds a fuzzy baby robin with a nest nearby, while a momma bird sits a few inches up the branch, feeding a plump caterpillar to another baby bird, already out of the nest, its wings but stubs, but still with a little beak craned wide open to receive.

And the prayer itself, read to me, then later read *by* me, introduced a vaster tenderness behind the snug scene.

Dear Father,
  hear and bless
Thy beasts
  and singing birds;
And guard
  with tenderness
Small things
  that have no words.[21]

"*Dear* Father," the prayer began, I notice now. Might that little word before the heavenly Father's name have left an impression? Here is an echo of Julian of Norwich's *Dearworthy.* I think children are more attuned to such realities than we may think. They come out with minor profundities before they can read and write. When my grandson Elias was tiny, he said the Lord's Prayer in this way: "Our Father, who art in heaven, hallowed be my name." Well, not exactly right—the *my* instead of *thy*—but he captured something of the honor and dignity with which God invested humankind.

We persons are made, as Genesis famously says, in the image of God. I think even a child can begin to catch what that might mean. As an adult, I can see how it tells us that we reflect the divine intelligence, God's will, and creativity. But even more, because we have been created, by some daily miracle we move around under more than what some see as the universe's dark, hollow sky; we are, to our core, made with some of the personalness that stooped to making and tending.

THE GOD WHO CREATES AND CARES

When God created alps and oceans and woodland owls, according to the biblical account, he said, "Let there *be* . . ." But when it comes to our making, it is "Let us *make*." To speak about making uses a verb that is more active, dynamic, and involved. Here the Trinity helps me see even more. Not only does God exist, but God has a delightful time making things. To create only befits a triune being who overflows with life and love.

God seemed to enjoy setting off fireworks of creativity—not for sport but for the possibilities of relating. The sparkling majesty of meteor showers pales next to the way he showers human life with kindness. To speak of the Trinity is to say that the great, vast God of all draws close and cares for you and me. It's another way to say, "God is love," a verse that prefaces this with "and so we know and rely on the love God has for us."[22] Here we see a God who is not only infinite but Someone a child might feel invited to address as *Dear*. As a Father.

To speak of the Trinity is to say that the great, vast God of all draws close and cares for you and me.

In the ancient world, this was astonishing news. In one old creation story, the Mesopotamian "Enuma Elish," the gods fight, and the victors make the losing divinities their slaves. Tired of the abject work, one goddess creates humans to take over the hard labor. And while these humans are made from clay, like Adam in the Bible, they aren't honored with a name—they are anonymous workers. It's all very impersonal. Worse, the gods in that story act moody, careless, and even hostile toward humans. They have high-maintenance needs.

Compare that to Genesis. God creates Adam and Eve with attention and love. This deity gives the first couple names and treats them with care, even after they disobey. The Creator keeps hanging around the neighborhood. Doesn't get flummoxed or decide to back off.

The idols of Israel's pagan neighbors—their false gods—couldn't act or help, as Psalm 115 taunts:

They have mouths, but cannot speak,
eyes, but cannot see.
They have ears, but cannot hear,
noses, but cannot smell.
They have hands, but cannot feel, . . .
nor can they utter a sound with their throats.[23]

Next to these fickle or passive idols, what a relief: a heavenly Being, robed in glory, who makes, sees, speaks, and even feels.[24] And while God showed special affection for Israel, again and again, God stressed that he is Creator of all people, that that affection overflows to every nation, tribe, and people. That would be you and me, not to put too fine a point on it.

I like how Paul J. Pastor described creation as a "world utterly founded on love."[25] God wants us around. God is eager to hear us talk. God constantly invites us to know him better, to relate more deeply and contentedly. God even offers *kinship*—an old-fashioned word for connection, one that comes from the same historical root as our word *kindness*.

Those early hearers of the biblical creation accounts, especially any pagans in the audience, must have been rocked back on their heels. Kindness and kinship? From the scary gods of thunder and moody nights? Wouldn't that seem too good to be true? Yet some of them did see something attractive in Israel's God. They wanted what the prophets called *steadfast love*, what the New Testament would eventually call *grace*. I wonder how your early experiences of God's presence left you. Did you feel drawn closer? Or did you worry that God was mad at you, frustrated that you weren't doing "better"? Or maybe you felt God was faraway and uninvolved.

It's a perennial temptation. There would be a revival of that latter view of a stand-offish deity in more modern times. Deism, as a philosophical movement, as some of us remember from high school history classes, had its heyday during the American Revolution. Deists stressed that God does not intervene in the world he created. God is most like a watchmaker who built the universe, wound it up like an old-fashioned clock, and then retired. Or went off to other exploits.

I share this bit of history because I still see its effects. I think of my own upbringing in an established denomination and suburban church. We absorbed an approach to piety that stressed formality. We heard calls from the pulpit to be decent people who love our neighbors. But was this God too kind, too gentle, to overwhelm me with grandeur or leave me awestruck by his beauty and power?

God isn't some overly sweet, sentimental figure. For one thing, God exists fully and completely in and of and from God's very self.[26] God needs nothing from us to be God. And this God aches for justice. Sides with those who are sinned against. Here is a Spirit who comes as a mighty wind. Here is a Jesus who overturns the tables of the moneychangers in the temple. It's possible to so emphasize the God of grace that we lose sight of the biblical call to please God. Trying to love God with heart, soul, mind, and strength and working to love our neighbor as ourself, as Jesus called us to, has a way of making us humble.

At the same time, this impressive God who calls us to faithfulness becomes intimate. The Trinity helps us avoid two extremes: thinking of God as too soft and mild, or as too distant to reach out to us. In it we see both an open invitation of grace and the chance to be transformed by love.

Growing up, I didn't hear much about the encounter possible through a vibrant faith. What I did see of God—though I didn't fully understand—was a kindly figure never eager to punish. My church didn't try to scare or pressure people. I wasn't traumatized by intimidating or threatening sermons like some others were. And for that, I'm grateful.

With the Trinity, however, we watch a story unfold where more is at stake than pleasant feelings after sitting in a pew for an hour. There's drama here. This living God commits fully to the world he made, never distant or stand-offish. Within God's very Self we glimpse an outgoing relational movement, a conversation with us born of love and hope. Which lays upon us some responsibility. He is supremely involved in the world he makes and wants us involved too. For that same love reaches out—catches us up in that movement toward others. This living God engages against that which opposes God and wants to subvert the good. We get front-row seats for the unfolding of all kinds of action. Action that keeps the creation moving toward further good.

This living God commits fully to the world he made, never distant or stand-offish.

Which makes the theater of creation all the more astonishing as a gift. If God doesn't need us but still wants us simply out of generosity, we gain a new glimpse of the universe's order and reliability. We see a divine trustworthiness behind it. A *steadfast* love. Vocabulary like *sturdy* and *unshakable* applies. Theologians talk about God as *immutable*, unchanging and not reliant on our advice to know what to do next. God's changelessness does not suggest monotony or lovelessness but rather a steadfast, burning constancy. Did you, perhaps, trigger an impatient parent while growing up? Did you face bursts of irritation when you disappointed someone?

Here in creation, we see God's love as steady action—not reaction. This love does not fluctuate or fly off the handle. In this classical doctrine that buttresses God's eternal steadiness in complicated language, we see a constant kindness, a commitment to us. *Covenant* is a big word in the Bible. It refers to God's faithful promise to care. And God enlists us in this work of justice being established in the world's broken places and unjust situations.

More good news: Looking back, I see that my starry brush with the heavenly realm was not an invitation to a submersion into some vast oneness. The interconnectedness of creation does not mean each person becomes a drop in an oceanic limitlessness, a speck merging into cosmic vastness. These pictures seem to exhaust some folks' view of God these days. But God's loving attention to human persons means we have a role to play in the lives of others around us, whom God likewise cares about.

CREATOR, SUSTAINER, AND MORE

If there's something tender in such naming of God—a personalizing in the persons of the Trinity—there is also clarity, layers of deeper meaning. Which means we lose something when we grasp for substitutes, as sometimes happens in mainline church circles. I mean a common recourse to naming the Trinity's God—as Creator, Sustainer, and Sanctifier. Yes, such vocabulary avoids limiting God to any hint of gender. But that naming doesn't convey the same richness. The Trinity is not about God's job description. It's not just assigning tasks to the Three. It's more personal than that.

The other day, I read an evolutionary anthropologist making the case that, among all our animal relatives, only humans have fathers that stay around after birth, invested and empathic and involved. I can't vouch for the science of that statement, and a friend noted right off that it doesn't apply to nesting birds. Still, it seems supremely human to expect a parental presence and, when it is missing or overlooked, to mourn its absence. We are more than interested in affection; we are driven by it, maddened by its lack. And we can draw on Scripture for an enriching range of images but still enlist the highest intimacy. Even before the New Testament's revelation of the triune God, we got hints of how much was possible.

Isaiah exulted as he spoke to Israel, his people with whom God made a covenant,

> *You will nurse and be carried on her arm*
> *and dandled on her knees, [says the Lord].*
> *As a mother comforts her child,*
> *so will I comfort you.*[27]

Jesus told us to address God as Father—*our* Father.[28] And then we see him calling on God as *Abba,* a term for an affectionate father, not unlike our "Dad." And not just Jesus is to say that name! The apostle Paul spoke of our own praying in that way: "We cry out . . . 'Abba, Father.'"[29] And later in the Christian tradition, Julian, delighted by God's fatherlike care, and likely a mother herself, wrote, "When [a child] is distressed and frightened, it runs quickly to its mother; and if it can do no more, it calls to the mother for help with all its might."[30] Or the Puritan pastor, Richard Sibbes, writing centuries ago, said, "Such a goodness is in God as is in a fountain, or in the breast that loves to ease itself of milk."[31]

And there's more family imagery too. The New Testament turns also to the language of adoption. God "destined us for adoption as his children through Jesus Christ, according to the good pleasure of his will."[32] Adoption as his children? Whatever our wandering as cosmic orphans, God wants to bring us fully into his family.

BEYOND ALL ANALOGIES

But something interesting emerges here, all the more striking given the imagery of family and parental intimacy. While the Bible gives us images time and again, it uses metaphors for the Trinity sparingly.

Anyone who has taught Sunday school knows the temptation

to reach for simple analogies—like an egg: shell, white, yolk. The problem is how impersonal, even mechanical, these images seem. I'm after better, more vivid ways to picture the Trinity. For we ponder the three living in intimacy, how they work in us and the world, or relate in delight as they create and sustain. Better to speak of how at the heart of it all is not just a Creator but one who commits to us, who makes covenant. Who promises effervescent, ever-living compassion. Who seeks us even when we feel left out or stand at a distance, longing for a home we cannot enter.

No wonder ancient Augustine preached often on the story commonly called the parable of the prodigal son, better titled the story of the Father's extravagant love.[33] He returned to it repeatedly—the story Jesus told of a wayward son and the exuberant love of his father when the son came back from his dissolute life—likely thinking of his own eros, his own errors, and his flight from purity that pulled him further from the God he ultimately wanted to meet. But it was more than a picture of the prodigal, errant son that drew him. Augustine lingered on Jesus' story of an earthly father's wildly abundant mercy, the true star of the story. He must have seen the open arms of the Father's embrace as a picture full of meaning—for himself, for others, for all—a grace and mercy revealed astonishingly in the coming of the Son of God.

For Augustine, it was more than a cozy story. "Every child looking for an absent, distant father," wrote James K. A. Smith about his own absent father in parallel to Augustine's dad hovering in the shadows, "is on the road to cover up a deeper desire: that such a father would come looking for them—that the arrow of hunger would be reversed and the father would return."[34] I know that sense of absence from my own father, who was kind but not exactly eager to spend a lot of time with me.

One night Dad and Kevin were watching some TV show at my bedtime. In my jammies, I made my way to both couches where they were sprawled, eyes glued on *Get Smart*, barely noticing my good night kiss. It would be one of the last times I kissed my dad good night. I sensed, from his nonverbal signals, that maybe I had outgrown this ritual. Not that he acted unkindly or off-puttingly—just that it might be time for something else. It occurs to me now that maybe he didn't intend to send that message, that any awkwardness was, well, in me. How could I know? Sometimes we don't.

But Augustine kept searching, as so many of us do when bereft of parental security. Ambrose, a revered bishop and imposing figure, mentored Augustine through his friendship and kindnesses—not just his sermons—and doing so tipped his young admirer over the edge into obedience and belief. We often look for father figures, don't we? Or mothers we never had. The personal attention the elder paid the young seeker finally helped Augustine open himself to a merciful God of grace. Ambrose was a fount of warmth. A little like God himself.

It is God—God in the delighted communion of the Trinity—for Augustine, for me, and for many others, who forms the ultimate draw.

GOD DOESN'T MAKE JUNK

I picture myself a bit older, seeing a poster on a bulletin board or classroom door—maybe at church. It grew out of activism for racial justice and depicted an African American child against an urban neighborhood backdrop. The caption read: "God doesn't make junk." I'm sure its poking at any notion of white superiority wasn't lost on me. But it struck me in another way too: If God created the world in a mysterious way, then I could see how even I, just a child, had worth, shaped by the hands of a creative God. The mystery, the vastness, even the evening's glowing beauty mattered but so did the quiet recognition that I could be treasured, even loved.

No human can love that perfectly—father or mother. Still, it is hard to imagine a more intimate word to describe a father's caring involvement than *love*. Or a mother's. Reading Augustine while working on this book, I recognized my barely registered, perhaps submerged, missing of a dad's intimacy. Did I begin to wonder, going to Sunday school, whether that hole could have been filled by a celestial love and compassion?

This morning, as I wrote, a Bible verse I've come across struck me differently than it ever has before. The apostle Paul convinced the church under his care in Galatia that they didn't need to earn God's love through moralistic schemes or ritual hoops: "And because you are children, God has sent the Spirit of his Son into our hearts, crying, 'Abba! Father!'"[35]

Something deep in me felt assured. Here was a glimpse of God's tenderness—not only toward the world but also directed to me, to people like you and me. The passage expresses the fullness of the Trinity: God the Father, the Son, the Spirit—the heavenly gang's all there. More significant, these names for God appear together, inviting us to know and feel God's tenderness. The Spirit, called the Spirit of the Son—the Holy Spirit—God sends into our hearts, prompting us to call on God, to *cry out* to God. The apostle guides us toward a term of affection: *Papa*.

This is not a prayer we might naturally think up. It's too intimate. But the Spirit moves in us, prompting a confidence we might not muster on our own, especially on days we feel unworthy.

It's a good thing—given our tendency to fall away, feel far from God, or sometimes ignore God—that we can recognize yet another aspect of our condition before the Trinity. Not just our occasional need for help, forgiveness, or reassurance but the chasm of our distance. Our need, all the more, to turn to a merciful God for merciful rescue.

FOUR

WHAT HAPPENED, UNRULY HEART?

Love bade me welcome. Yet my soul drew back.
—George Herbert

Almighty God, you alone can bring into order the unruly wills and affections of sinners.
—*The Book of Common Prayer*

AS THE SAYING GOES, THERE WAS MORE TO THE PICTURE than just the wall behind it. Even a little drama.

In the photo I'm smiling, pushing myself up from my tummy on my baby-fat-laden forearms. Someone off-camera—Mom or Dad, maybe a very enthusiastic stranger—caught my attention. My parents kept the tarnished gold-framed picture on their dresser throughout my childhood. You can tell that I was loving the attention, staring out at the world with an infant's inquisitive eyes, hoping for a face to connect with. I'm showing a capacity for happy affection.

Maybe you, too, look at your baby photos and notice something.

Sometimes, with years of reflection, you see more than you did at first. In my imagination, I see how the camera could also have captured the next moment, my smile turned into a quivering lip as I realized I was in a strange place, taken from my mother's arms. Or maybe normal sibling stuff—pouting because I had to share attention with a brother standing in the background. And now, too late to check, I suddenly wonder, *Was my brother's baby photo standing tall on the same dresser top?*

In the photo, I see how I sent out signals—what psychologists call bids for connection—testing the world in which I found myself, getting a sense of the place I'd landed. Would I get what I wanted and needed? Would my little sphere prove secure? No child escapes wondering—especially when things seem random or heart-rending: A parent breaks a promise. A child in the nursery wallops us. Instead of being told we're loved, we get yelled at. The little soul's desire to be loved plays out in an imperfect world, among imperfect people. If you spend any time reflecting, I don't have to work to make a case.

And children themselves, as we all know, aren't immune from getting jealous and crabby and grabby. I cannot imagine I always behaved like an angel in cute footie pajamas. Even from the earliest days, there was something . . . well, less than pure. No matter how young, alongside the glory of being a created person, the dignity and mystery, there is less than crystalline purity. Our mini ego elbows its way to the front and center. We fail to show love. When older, we pick on a neighborhood kid. Or we struggle not to hit back, stomp out, or slink away in mopey silence when everything in us wants to. So what happens when we bring to God's offer of loving-kindness our own flawed, imperfect selves?

Amid all the influences around me, I wasn't just getting up every morning to play or get read to, or eat Cheerios, or, when older, hustle to school. With the kids in the neighborhood, Saturday cartoons, Sunday school, all those ads, and all my feelings, I had some figuring out to do. Who would help me know what mattered and what didn't, what would hurt a classmate's feelings or show kindness?

Questions come up as we wade through the waters of our beginnings: Why did I do what I knew I shouldn't, or refuse to do what I sensed I should? And what do we do with our regrets when we fail? Even a child can know when she messes up big-time, hurting others needlessly. Acts in defiance of the good.

This is a serious challenge in our standing before God as we move into more self-awareness. We exist in a situation where, based on our lack, we need more than we can come up with on our own. "Surely I was sinful at birth," wrote David in a psalm, "sinful from the time my mother conceived me."[1] We call out for mercy and assistance.

Here I see a connection in the Trinity—the great promise to address our common human condition, mending the habitual ways we stray and opt for self over others, over God.

This condition is a matter of more than an occasional "Oops!" It is not a rare lapse but, as someone put it, "a full-time career choice."

"NAUGHTIES IN MY BADNESS"

Jill was getting exasperated with our then-three-year-old daughter one afternoon. Finally, in frustration, she said, "Bekah, why did you do that?!"

What Bekah said has become part of our family lore. Without a pause, she said, "I guess I have naughties in my badness."

We all carry a bentness. An irresistible gravity of self-involvement. An inclination toward "badness" that explains the more visible naughtiness or lapses. There's a Latin phrase that captures this: *Incurvatus in se.* That means you and I are turned or curved inward on ourselves. It points to how we live inward toward self and away from God.[2] Sometimes what should be our love for others reverses course, like a river's currents, flowing back toward the self—ourselves—so quietly we barely notice.

I saw a sign at a home goods store that seems to sum up this mindset: "Be you. Do you. For you." But maturing means finding your way out of the immersion in a deep-end pool of consuming self-attention. When I look back on my life, I see a living confirmation that not only are desires natural, they also become confused and disordered, driven by what *The Book of Common Prayer* calls our "unruly wills and affections."[3] We learn only partially to resist the temptation to enthrone the self above every other preoccupation.

I don't mean that self-abasement or self-loathing, religious or otherwise, has any place. Religion can traumatize, instill terror when it tries too hard to convince people of their fallenness and need for grace.

But we do know something doesn't work. Goodness doesn't always win out—in others or in us. "I do not understand what I do," wrote the apostle Paul, admitting the lure and power of wrongdoing. "For what I want to do I do not do, but what I hate I do."[4]

One historical figure struggled mightily with this reality. The church reformer Martin Luther, frustrated with his own failures, observed that the human person universally "so curved in" on itself that it uses everything within reach for its own purposes.[5] Luther quoted Jeremiah 17:9: "The heart is deceitful above all things, and desperately sick; who can understand it?"[6] I know, not exactly a welcome-to-my-happy-place pastoral scene. Grim, even.

This could still be true.

The forces that plague our souls have a perverse tenacity. They are not merely something we happen into. British writer Francis Spufford noted, "[It] is not just our tendency to lurch and stumble and screw up by accident, our passive role. . . . It's our active inclination to break stuff, 'stuff' here including moods, promises, relationships we care about, and our own well-being and other people's."[7]

This insight explains much of what confuses us and sometimes overwhelms us. We look around at incalculable cruelty in the world or recognize puzzling, persistent choices within ourselves that hurt us and others. Our self-consumed sin makes it harder to connect across relational chasms.

At the same time, the Trinity addresses our need for intimacy and restored relationships. It offers a way for reconciliation and mercy—a help that restores what is separated and broken. "You can't self-help your way out of this," James K. A. Smith said of our predicament of self-immersion.[8]

The Bible doesn't describe our tendency to do wrong as a few smudges on an otherwise white sheet of paper, or a checklist of teeny-tiny slip-ups. Instead, it speaks of something more serious: *sin*, a word that may make you uneasy, perhaps because you've heard it shouted from a platform or brandished like an emotional weapon rather than explained with care. Maybe such language makes your anxiety rise or your self-worth feel shaky. That word, though, points to a condition that runs through all of us, touching every life, every heart, the entire human race.

The disobedience of Adam and Eve in the primordial garden holds the sorry, beautiful world in its grip, even now. Holds *us*. If the fall of humankind was personal, it's also chronically communal. Our root captivity to sin passes from imperfect parent to imperfect child, generation to generation. As a species, we share in the disobedience of Adam and Eve in a headlong fall from paradise. And it comes with a boatload of fear. A fear that, rather than drive us from God, can draw us closer in.

A CROAK FOR A PRAYER

I hadn't noticed it till recently. The first prayer recorded in the Bible is a croak, a cowering, pitiable utterance. We hear Adam, speaking from hiding, hesitant. I can imagine him practically stuttering. When the harmony of the garden shattered and sin entered the world through Adam and Eve's disobedience, they slunk away, ashamed. Adam knew that the blissful communion of Eden had been shuttered. The fall had come between him and God.

Still, Genesis tells us, God asked Adam where he and Eve had gone off to: "Where are you?"

"I heard your voice in the garden," Adam answered, "and I was afraid because I was naked; and I hid myself."[9]

Hardly auspicious, this glimpse of primal conversation with God. But apt. Humankind's first prayer—Adam's prayer—quavers with pathos. Only recently have I recognized the poignancy in this scene—an essential prologue explaining the drama to come. Here we find illumination for our sorrows, our screwups, and our wobbly steps forward.

Relating to God now, and for all time, will contain an element of uncertainty and insecurity for humankind. No wonder I struggle to pray some days. No wonder our own conversations with God feel troubled, sporadic, even spasmodic. No wonder we turn away some days or cower. No wonder we feel distant from God. No wonder we experience a push-pull—drawing close and pulling back, our longing and defiance in a jumble, all while we make our way through the jagged edges of a broken world. The bewilderment caused by the rupture of sin affects our sense of what's possible when we think of God, much less want to talk with God or listen for what we hope is his voice.

All is not lost, of course. God earnestly preserves the order of things that Adam's disobedience threw off track. More on that later. Indeed, *God* is the one who's gone searching in this elemental scene in Genesis, not the first couple. The word for "where" in this text conveys a saddened, "Why are you not *here*?" God asked them, "Where are you?"—the Bible's first question—not because the Almighty was in the dark, but to say, with something like an ache, *Where have you gone?* Rabbi Rashi noted that God asked Adam, not because God didn't *know* but to invite Adam to speak, to reply. This offers hope for this less-than-impressive first glimpse of prayer, in itself.

The bewilderment caused by the rupture of sin affects our sense of what's possible when we think of God, much less want to talk with God or listen for what we hope is his voice.

Christian teachers often call this "fall" a tumble into original sin. For something emerges here that clarifies the Trinity's picturing of grace. The text shows more than sin and death entering the world through the one great trespass; it also points to a separation where there had been closeness, suffering where there had been a garden of delight. It introduces the chronic pain of social and relational distance. As Paul the apostle would later describe it, "the whole creation groans."[10] Those aching pangs of labor come bundled with the package, what Rowan Williams called the current "sphere of poverty, tears, loneliness, disillusion and the scars of countless unintelligible hurts."[11]

All this means much of our praying and living takes place amid a massive sense of in-betweenness—between human moral frailty and some kind of redemption. No wonder all humanity stumbles; we live with a proneness to *fall*, and we sometimes hurriedly scan our daily distractions in search of hiding places or soothing diversions.

I wonder how such a dark picture affects you. Maybe it comes to mind when you get sucked into "doomscrolling." I think of mornings when I read the news and my prayers are as much sighs as discourses. Can the suffering across the world get any worse? I think of grieving with social-distanced loneliness, missing those closest to me in those COVID days of safeguarding isolation. Times when I long for God to show up amid the strife between family members. Or when racial inequity still seems to be a wearying constant. Globally, there's genocide, for goodness' sake.

We have moments of painful glimpses of clarity, when everything around us and within us seems very far from what should be, the way it could be. We experience—sometimes viscerally—distances not only between humankind and God but between ourselves and others.

Lest we feel tempted always to shunt blame onto others, the Christian view of God and humanity reminds us: The problem is not only "out there." Inescapably, we have a part.

FICKLE SAINT AUGUSTINE

Augustine did some inventorying of his life, thinking of his own fickleness. He looked back without flinching. He began at life's early moments: childhood jealousies, for instance—though at times he judged himself too harshly, I'd argue. Augustine felt a compulsion to include in his accounting of his life his delight in transgression as a teen, like when he stole pears from an orchard with friends for nothing more than the sheer thrill of doing wrong. He had trouble quite figuring out why.

And so he prayed with an ache that communicates across all these centuries: "Such was my heart, O God, such was my heart. You had pity on it when it was at the bottom of the abyss. Now let my heart tell you what it was seeking there in that I became evil for no reason. I had no motive for my wickedness except wickedness itself. It was foul, and I loved it."[12] And Augustine looked inward unflinchingly at every stage in his life.

I can almost see him shaking his head as he wrote, repeating, "Such was my heart, O God, such was my heart." No wonder that, when we get honest, we identify with this ancient figure.

I've struggled with subtler forms of this curving inward. I mean an innate and inordinate need for approval and acceptance. Self-esteem has its place, to be sure. And of course, what child doesn't long for a parent to notice? I demonstrated this in my baby photography session—"Watch me!" is the watchword of childhood. Learning to read, being seen crossing the finish line at the track meet, singing in the school musical, getting passable grades: Yes, a child can expect to be noticed and commended. But as we mature, shouldn't a healthy person need fewer "likes" online? Less lost sleep stressing over accolades at the office? More freedom from needing a high standing among our peers? Elizabeth Oldfield wrote, "As infants, searching for another's gaze, scanning for the attentive eyes of a parent, mirror our search for the gaze of others throughout life."[13]

But even here I found a way to make a healthy thing crooked. Affirmation can become an obsession. Constantly boosting self-esteem has a downside if it leaves kids vaguely self-absorbed, unprepared to face challenges, dependent on praise, full of the accomplishments of the surface self. "Receiving attention and affirmation from the people around me is a lovely thing," said Oldfield, "but making it the ground for my sense of self is dangerous. I can find myself playing roles in their stories, as well as they in mine, and their own search for a stable identity colors our relationship."[14]

TOO GOOD FOR MY OWN GOOD

As for me, in our relational web at home, I was mostly the pliant child, the "good" boy, the one eager to please, my brother the one to thrash out at limits, buck convention. I *seemed* so selfless. If my neediness for warmth and approval meant I sacrificed some of my own aims, it also meant I pulled to myself the affection circulating in the system, sucked up more than my share, and left my brother grasping if not gasping for his share of the emotional goods getting passed around. I could read the room—to my benefit. *I'm sorry, Kevin, that I sided against you when you got, as our parents said, "rebellious."*

The seventies counterculture gave you plenty to work with! I was drawn, too, to the smells of living room incense and the crazy bell bottoms and the propulsive music, the idealism. I stayed in line, though. Didn't shake things up. But I was no perfect angel, for all I learned to lean hard on a natural knack for "niceness," cloaking faults in a shimmer of seeming kindness. It can look like humility incarnate when what you are doing is canvassing for sympathy or approval.

And that habit backfired. "We hope you will never disappoint us like Kevin did," my mom once cautioned when I was a teenager, well before Jill was in the picture. She dealt out of a deck heavy with guilt cards, sensing my vulnerability and eagerness. Looking back, it seems to me now like a way to insist I stay close. Did an inordinate need for affirmation make me more vulnerable to such gambits?

Even now, after all the years since being the adorable baby in that photo, I still often find myself focused on my own needs. Sometimes under my niceness and attention to appearances lurks an inner world of envy and outsized ambition. I'm too sensitive to slights and little ways people routinely don't shower everybody around them (uh, that would be me) with props. Under my friendly smile and fixation with looking good, I sometimes lapse into petty thoughts about people that would embarrass me if they knew. I doubt my belovedness so often that it robs me of joy and generosity.

WHEN COMPETING REPLACES COMMUNION

The fall of the human race in the garden of Eden was not only a flaunting of God's instruction and warning; it also plunged creation into a world of separation and distance from other people. In a world that often seems on fire, here is where we all find ourselves, every day. Sin introduced into the world a nagging desire on our part to compare and compete. We deflect when we could self-reflect. Adam not only hid from God behind proverbial fig leaves, he also pointed at Eve, trying to shift blame. There's "enmity between" the man and the woman. The pure harmony was ruptured forever.[15] Something in us fans to flames the temptation to push against another. We lash out in fear.

Sin introduced into the world a nagging desire on our part to compare and compete. We deflect when we could self-reflect.

You can explain a world of conflict this way. "What causes fights and quarrels among you?" asked the New Testament apostle James. He didn't answer his own question by pointing to geopolitical tensions (though those cannot be ignored). "Don't they come from your desires that battle within you? You desire but do not have, so you kill. You covet but you cannot get what you want, so you quarrel and fight."[16] We insist on self and ignore the harms we cause other selves. We desire more when we cannot find ourselves content to be loved in all the fullness God offers.

And it happens right where we live, not just a continent or ocean away. Parents know how much self gets in the way of our wanting *selflessly* to love our kids. For that matter, kids trying to love difficult parents know it too. As wonderful as marriage can be, anyone knows how much work it takes to keep it strong, so powerful are the emotions and defenses that would turn us inward and unleash our frustrations outward. How easy it becomes to snipe at each other. A single sharp remark can spark a response in kind, leading to our returned volley, becoming a cycle of escalating tension.

I recall a time Jill and I weathered a conflict. She had criticized me, or so it felt to me; she thought she was merely commenting on my not having cleaned up after myself in the kitchen. "I just got home from a long day," I shot back. But the problem wasn't just what I said. It was also that I glared at her, my face, I'm sure, hardened, the decibels of my voice climbing. Jill began to wither under the barrage of my impatience. Only when she practically brimmed with tears did I pull back the blistering anger. Only later, after we clicked off our bedside lamps, did Jill finally venture to say something out of the darkness. "I felt like you *turned* on me," she said in a wounded tone. I don't think I've ever heard her use that phrase, and it struck me, even while I found some words to apologize that I had bruised her spirit. It was later that the choice of words hit me. "Turned *on* me," she said. Not turned *toward* to be near. *On* me—as if to hurt, to do harm.

Our persistent natures don't just trip us up. They also wound others, whether family members close to us or communities further afield. They break down community. Sin plants distance, marring the harmony of creation. Strong currents pull us into the small world of self, often without us realizing it.

My friend Tim Taylor, a pastor, once put it this way, how we can bruise and damage others: "My autobiography has been a series of self-serving incidents. There I was, thoughtlessly bumping into folks here and there, totally unaware of what I was doing or who I was hurting." And, he felt, he added, alluding to the apostle Paul's talk about our trespasses leaving us lifeless, "dead in my sins." But Tim said all this with a bit of a chuckle; not that he didn't regret the bumps—the damage he had inflicted—but he was so full of joy that in Christ all this was being redeemed. He had found new life. The Tim Taylor I've come to know is wonderfully kind.[17]

The prayer for the season of Lent in *The Book of Common Prayer* helps here: "Almighty God, you know that we have no power in ourselves to help ourselves. . . ."[18] How dependent we are on God's forgiving grace and help. Resolve and better resolutions won't cut it. A list of better choices won't make us pristine and like a self-driving car. You could say it takes a Trinity to effect the rescue, so established are we in these self-enforcing patterns. It takes what Paul called "the grace of the Lord Jesus Christ, and the love of God, and the fellowship of the Holy Spirit."[19] Who doesn't need help from them all, the whole fellowship of the Three? True selfless love comes from beyond ourselves. We are dependent on the grace of God. Always. The grace of Christ. The community-building power of the Holy Spirit.

WRATH AS MEDICINE, NOT MALICE

There's help here—resources that make us able, in turn, to be more than we could be to others on our own.

This makes me think of how Christians sometimes seem to others who are outside the faith, looking in. Some Christians make poor advertisements for the love of God that's been offered to them. They may convey, perhaps unwittingly, a God who is just plain malicious. One who cruelly pursues sin and the sinner. Did you perhaps grow up under such judgey messages? If so, it might affect you to this day. And if you perpetuate them, you risk being off-putting to those who need mercy. Most people want little of this stern God.

I am not proposing a chumminess with One who is Almighty and personified Purity. He may allow difficult consequences to come our way, but never as ends in themselves—always with a view to our waking up to reconciliation. He allows the world's wrongdoers to have their freedom, but as the Bible says, he will not be mocked. He is no pushover and, given how intractable and cruel the world's injustices seem, I'm glad.

But he is also not petty. We remember that God always, even in judgment, ultimately desires good. "The language used regarding the wrath of God is to be understood figuratively," wrote the second-century theologian Origen, "for it is as if one were to call the words of a physician 'threats,' when he tells his patients, 'I will have to use the knife, and apply cauteries, if you do not obey my prescriptions, and regulate your diet and mode of life in such a way as I direct you.'"[20]

God may discipline us, but it always comes as medicine, never meanness. God does not strike people with cancer, he does not "take" our loved ones, he does not start wars to punish pagans or send tsunamis to drown sinners. At the same time, he warns us that certain paths lead to particular ends. "God is the only comfort," wrote C. S. Lewis. He can seem like a terror, he goes on: like "the thing we need most and the thing we most want to hide from." But, Lewis said, while we may be tempted to put ourselves at odds with God, God "is our only possible ally."[21]

And we recall that our sin need not separate us from a love so lavish and constant. Repentance takes place at God's invitation, with God's promise to show mercy. He runs toward those he loves, as Jesus' parable of the two sons showed.

God may discipline us, but it always comes as medicine, never meanness.

We also remember that God will bring justice. God will reorder the disorder of sin. Wrath in that sense paints a picture of a God who wants the world's ultimate good and is willing to upset some apple carts—or money-changing tables in the temple—to achieve it.

NO, WE CAN'T DO IT ALL BY OURSELVES

There's need for humility here. I hope that is what you, reader, are sensing. Not condemnation. Not beating up on yourself. But rather a new determination of dependence. When the early Christians thought about their experience of God, they knew the limits of what they could orchestrate—the folly of favor on demand. Something about the Trinity drew them in but also remained too mysterious for them to presume upon. Knowing the grace that redeemed them and brought them back home to God, they made it a priority to convey grace to others. A grace-shaped story of what God did to reach them kept them from feeling cocky.

The God of the Trinity, overflowing in grace, the one through Jesus we call *Abba,* Father, and who, through the Holy Spirit, embraces us in prayer—became their rescue (about which I will say more later). I like what Chris Wheeler said about how he loves the idea of resolutions—who wouldn't, he mused, want not to get better as a husband, father, writer, human? "But," he confessed, "I also know how long a year is. I've been spinning around the earth's axis long enough to know that my motivations are tilted, my will is eclipsed, and my abilities are gravity-bound."[22]

Augustine also knew, given the seriousness of the situation, how ingrained some of our interior habits are. He would be the first to stand up in a room to say we need a divine load of help. It's not just reformation; it's rescue. Not just forgiveness but the refashioning of what has become shriveled and diseased. And the good news is this: Broken as we are, as broken as our situations are, transformation still happens. Hope for something new appears on a horizon of

The good news is this: Broken as we are, as broken as our situations are, transformation still happens.

grace. We are not only accepted, we are fully beloved—through and through.

Maybe we see ourselves with a shudder of revulsion. We have moments we feel keenly that we have disappointed ourselves or others. I mean more than the fact that most of us see things about ourselves that annoy us. Many of us wrestle more profoundly. The situation seems more dire.

"I don't think," I heard a preacher say, "that people, for the most part, tend to like themselves." He was speaking from the vantage point of years of ministry, walking with people through their disappointments, temptations, and heartaches. They live with the pressure that comes from a restless, driven need to self-improve and, well, *prove* something. We know the feeling: "The embarrassment of a Christian I knew myself to be," as Kate Gaston put it wryly. "The final letdown in a long line of letdowns, and God was up there somewhere, shaking his head in mild, paternal disappointment."[23]

MORE THAN BEING LIKED—BEING LOVED

But all of us—for all our imagined baby cuteness, big-person accomplishments, or self-loathing—need more than affirmation from peers, friends, or even parents. We also need God's overflowing affection. Sometimes it's the littlest oversight that stings us, making us doubt whether we can be loved for who we are. But maybe it's also the "big" wrong, the thing we fear makes God mad, that separates us from the hope of mercy. We feel ashamed by what we've done and shouldn't or what we haven't done and should have. And we secretly, at least on our best days, pine not only for moral instruction but for transformation. Through the Trinity, God shows up with the patience of a father for his wayward children, the redeeming grace of Jesus our Savior, and the power of the Holy Spirit to make it real.

It's in situations like this where I see the Trinity as more than an interesting puzzle for our mere human curiosity. "Grace is the big relief at the heart of Christianity," said David Zahl.[24] Or, as Julian put it, with medieval flourish and elegance, "Our courteous Lord does not want his servants to despair even if they fall frequently and grievously. Our falling does not stop his loving us."[25] The Trinity is God in God's self, yes. But also an extended hope for what we could never do alone. Less like health food supplements and more like an emergency room intervention. Not a pleasant hobby but a lifeline, given how much is at stake.

I like how my friend Charlie Peacock puts this need: "As it turned out, [mere] transcendence as I understood it was not what I needed. . . . I needed real-time, earthbound rescue. I needed forgiving, reconciling, restorative love."[26] A love and a hope that does for us what we couldn't even dream of doing for ourselves.

I was talking to a good friend recently about the conviction that God loves humankind—not merely endures us, not just has a passing interest, but *truly loves* us. She was struggling not to be a skeptic. If this God does turn toward us as love personified, if such love is real, then why is there so much suffering, and why do we seem unable to stop it? She has wounds from a distant mother, a member of a family who, like my parents, would quickly cut off contact for imagined slights. Such experiences take more than inspirational slogans. More than self-help reminders to think positively.

In the Trinity, the Bible says, we see a God who doesn't simply love but—on every level possible—*is* love. Who draws astonishingly close in Christ. In every circumstance. When we say God made himself vulnerable by taking on flesh, that's what we mean. God took a chance when he appeared on earth as something as fragile and breakable as a human being. God took a terrible risk in coming to a place where sin reigns, without every possible protection of divine armor. For us and for our sake. But he did.

THE STING OF CORRECTION, THE HEALING OF LOVE

But maybe you realize, as I do, that things get complicated. Sometimes the growth in love meets challenges. It usually needs to lead to growth in holiness. Sometimes our sin catches up with us or those we love, no matter how loving God's work in the Trinity seems. We need ongoing reminders.

My parents would sometimes keep bottles of Coke in the fridge. Mom sternly told me not to sneak swallows. The idea was to save the carbonated sugar water for special occasions, when allowed to. I wasn't supposed to help myself. But I did. I would drink a little bit from a bottle and put it back.

One Saturday afternoon my mom confronted me. "Tim, did you drink out of the Coke bottle?"

"No," I said, wary.

But it was obvious that I had. There was no question that she could see that I'd gulped a little down.

I had also been caught in a lie.

My dad got called in. This was my punishment: He said, "Hold out your hand. Palm up." Then he took a belt and whacked my open hand. Not repeatedly, but—if I remember correctly—more than once.

It stung like crazy.

It's the only time I remember being disciplined in this way, though I suspect there were other times a belt got pulled out, compliant child though I mostly was. While harsh and never a practice I repeated with my own children, it was a lesson in consequence. A moral law exists for our flourishing and for the good of society, so it's not surprising that a sting might follow when we push it aside.

Maybe Augustine went over the top in his version of our life with God and with one another, veering toward self-loathing. But I'm drawn to the pathos, to his honest admittance of moral vulnerability. There's a corrective here in our day of extravagant self-esteem. We do need accountability. Our children do. Our leaders do. It's not in the scope of this book to treat the whole challenge of sin and retribution. But in the wider divine order, correction never comes from petulance or antsy impatience.

Grace is what matters most. The range of experiences we have—from being brought into the world, to being loved, to being rejected, to questioning our standing before God—find their fulfillment here. God somehow uses all that happens to us and in us to make us more responsive to grace, to make us even desperate for grace. We realize that bootstrapping has its limits. All the education or opportunity in the world will not mean we always make good choices. We might think we somehow stand apart from others, even look down on them, when in reality we all stand in need of grace. Mercy is unearned precisely because mercy is, well, *mercy.* It's a gift we don't deserve yet cannot do without.

And something else gives us hope. As Augustine came to a jolting sense of his own incompleteness, of our human inability to live fully for God or others, I see a defenselessness born of humility. We witness a forget-the-proprieties search for something to heal the queasiness born of his sin and self-wearying iniquity. He knew, as Rowan Williams said to me, "if we see ourselves as finished, if there's nothing more to long for, it's as if we are blocking off a pathway toward the deep source of our being, which is God."[27]

Perhaps Augustine's quest for what he found and missed in his home life led him to his holy unsettledness, his longing for moral goodness.

Maybe it formed the line for which he's most quoted throughout history: "Our hearts are restless, O God, until they find their rest in you."[28] If any ancient writer fashioned a prayer that achieved celebrity status, it would be Augustine.

This is the kind of insight that can point us forward in hope. It wasn't that Augustine peevishly could never be satisfied. I like that his mind and heart could not settle easily into complacency. Faith was no drowsy-making sleeping pill, no deadening tranquilizer to keep him from confronting his inner disasters, his compulsions to use people—especially women—as means only to gratification or self-satisfaction.

No, this does not downplay what he did wrong or failed to do. It shows that he sensed his constant need for God and God's help. God's forgiving love. And so he looked upward and outward and forward. And then he could boldly believe that God would receive him with the welcome reserved for a cherished child. He kept writing about it because he wanted others to experience this belonging he found in his own life story. It came to him in nothing less than a divine scale. Only the triune God's inexhaustibly rich possibilities to help and redeem could assuage what he restlessly sought.

For he preceded that prayer admitting his restlessness by confessing to God, "You have made us for yourself." Life does not come only from conception; it comes from divine making and keeping. "The mind is drawn by love," Augustine affirmed in his *Homilies on the Gospel of John*. Thus, he pleaded, "Give me a lover and he will know by experience what I am saying here. . . . Give me someone who is hungry . . . and he will know what I am saying."[29]

No dreary anti-worldliness here. This seems to make sense of how restlessness formed part of his genius—and part of my quest too. We look at, said Rowan Williams, Jesus the child. In an icon important to Eastern Orthodoxy, Rowan saw how God took our broken realities and predilection for sin seriously in the incarnation.

"Now when we look at God," wrote Rowan Williams, "we do not see only the terror and darkness, the cloud that brooded over Sinai [where God came and gave Moses the Ten Commandments]; we see Jesus, taking his throne on a mother's lap. . . . [He] has come closer to us than we are to our own selves, as one of the saints has said."[30]

Which is why the next section will spend so much time on that Son—the one who crawled into a mother's lap but whose mercies also changed the world. He brings the salve for the wound, the solid food that fills my soul's empty places, and the courage for intimacy to meet what the world might offer or withhold.

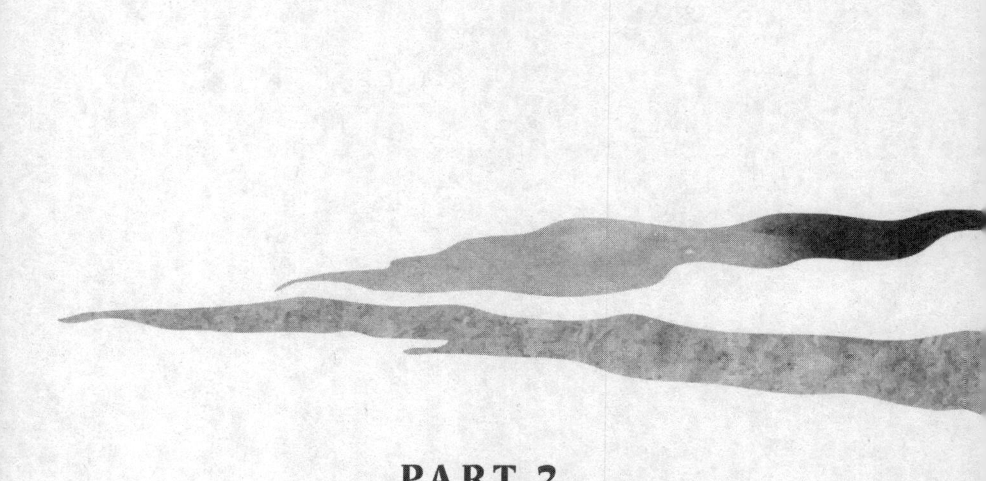

PART 2

OUR GOD HOLDS: THE SON

FIVE

WHERE IS A HAVEN FOR MY HEART?

You will nurse and be carried on her arm,
and dandled on [Jerusalem's] knees, [says the Lord].
As a mother comforts her child,
so will I comfort you.
—Isaiah 66:12–13

How often have I desired to gather your children
together as a hen gathers her brood under her wings.
—Jesus (Matthew 23:37 nrsv)

A SONG FROM MY CHILDHOOD NOW FEELS MORE LIKE A warning than a ballad. Not that I had a clue of its darker portents. When I toddled around, I was met with smiles. My brother would make me laugh at his silly-face antics. Mom would gather me into her arms.

The rocking chair where we sat remained a fixture in our house, and it is clear in my mind's eye: a spindle-back colonial, the honey-brown on the arms worn down to bare grain. It creaked in calming rhythm as we sat and communed.

And while her bony back pressed against the chair's stiff back, she made a comforting place for me as a child. Whatever my fears, I found an answer for the hunger all children feel for physical closeness. She crooned "I love 'ou," in a cooing baby talk and a drawl left over from her Tennessee childhood.

And she sang. I don't think I'm projecting backward when a memory of her visits me, and I picture her singing to me—the only time I heard her sing—certainly not hymns in church, where she stood, hymnal in hand, too shy to hum or mouth the words.

I imagine how the near-comic characters of the ballad "Froggy Went a Courtin'"[1] made her smile as we rocked. If she didn't sing it herself, I heard the song—indelibly—somewhere around the house, from the radio or a record.

Of all the quirky oddities of a tune for me to have stick in my mind!

But don't many of us have songs—a child's ditty, folk tunes, sometimes hymns—that transport us to an early moment, sparking a memory, insight, or longing? The lyrics can well up in memory to reassure us or help us to brave a fear. They may help form our faith. Talk of relational abundance in the Trinity will sound hollow without confronting what could and does happen in a broken world.

Froggy went a courtin' and he did ride, uh huh.

I can mentally picture Froggy in a rakish cap, his long, awkward legs about to spring. The conversation between a frog and a mouse sounded like a fairy tale—to a point. Whimsical, but what a little one finds playful can carry a deeper, almost prophetic weight. "The Strange Tale," as the original Scottish lyrics dating to the 1550s were called, I'd learn later, became popular in the American South, where my mom grew up. And still on airwaves and recordings in the late 1950s of my early life. Did I first hear it there?

The ballad would have taken its place along with other fables, like many of us heard—the *Grimm's Fairy Tales* volume I still have after all these years. Some of those stories are, well, *grim*. We picked up suspense and hints of danger. Maybe you were a little scared to hear Little Red Riding Hood find a maternal figure—supposedly her grandmother—turn menacing, turn *on* her, until the brave girl is rescued. Such storylines—sung, read, acted—spark our childlike imagination.

As a child I would have known only vaguely what courting meant. It doesn't sound like the main character of the ballad traipsed off to the nearby playground swing. He "rode right up to Miss Mouse's door . . . gave three raps and a very loud roar." I wonder what impression that scene made on me! The lyrics intimate a blustery romance. Mr. Frog's quest, like any interesting story, meets an obstacle or two. The beloved's reaction is a cool face turned to his eager proposal:

"Without my uncle Rat's consent," she replies, "I wouldn't marry the president."

And beyond the pair's feelings and desires, others held the fate of their affection in their grasp. Or thought they did. The winsome characters bump into the chance that someone will withhold consent, foreshadowing trouble from my mother.

And there were hints of a world with other threats: "Froggy went a courtin' . . . *sword and pistol by his side*."

Why would he even need weapons? The image of a frog, of all creatures, gearing up to go out with a sword and gun at the ready feels like more than just a random detail. It hints that this courtship might not unroll as you first expect. He might encounter someone who could threaten. He'd need some protection.

Words like that set a child in a wider world, where hard or scary things loom, where arguments can harm—where wild things live. In my school, our fourth-grade teachers might suddenly call, "Drop!" and we would scramble under desks into a fetal position, hands covering our vulnerable heads. "Duck and cover," I think the drills were called—no child's game, this. The backdrop was atomic war, the need for us to shield our heads and faces from dangers we could barely imagine. I can't recall what the teacher said by way of explanation. I couldn't have known the extent of the danger, but given the missiles pointing at us—and ours at "them"—we could have been incinerated. Do you remember some of the anxieties of being a child? Third graders participate now in active shooter drills, for Pete's sake.

It was natural for me to wonder at my surroundings. Children instinctively worry, as they grow, about whether or not they will tread a safe path through the world. Even in households with no violence, children from seemingly secure homes get pangs of disquiet: fear of creaking noises after lights out, fear of being reprimanded too harshly, shoved around at school, or ridiculed across a neighborhood fence. A predator creeps them out and causes deep harm. Some kids get pushed around, literally, because of their social status or racial background.

Such experiences are as old as humankind. Augustine, centuries ago, looked back on his own childhood, his difficult days in boarding school with cruel teachers, chiding God a bit: "I prayed that I would not be beaten, a prayer you did not see fit to answer."[2] Here reverence indulges in a touch of irony.

The stakes seem just as high or higher as we grow older. The uncertainties ever present. Will the world's harshness—to us—happen despite our longing for it not to?

THE WORD WHO HOLDS THE WORLD—AND US

We transplanted several times as I grew up—from Phoenix to Southern California, from apartments to houses, from renting to owning—and always the chair moved with us. And wherever we were when I was little, I would hop on and then off Mom's lap and go play again, sturdier, steadier than before, eager even if not always sure of myself. I still had normal fears but was ready to play and run. I wonder what article of furniture or special place made you feel safe as you grew into your own challenges.

Even when I outgrew the rocking chair, sometimes we would talk when I'd come in from playing. I could tell Mom of the next-door bully, an older, bigger boy who barred me from the playground slide I loved. Don't we all recall those times when someone was mean or threatening, when we battled anxieties?

Any talk of a God of love, a God revealed in the Trinity who *is* love, will falter if we ignore such realities or leave them out of the conversation. It's not just the little dramas, either.

The year I was born, that summer, mothers kept kids home from community pools, while at public schools, students received polio vaccines injected into their arms. Later, when I was in grade school, researchers created a vaccine-saturated sugar cube—a sweeter version. I remember standing in line to take mine. I don't think I had much idea what it protected me from.

And must I not have heard, passing a black-and-white screen in the living room tuned to network news, reports of war in far-off Asia, a national draft that in a few years would make my brother worry about being sent off? Of strife and ferment when a Montgomery,

Alabama, Black woman sat in the "White" section of a bus? When little Ruby Bridges, accompanied by federal marshals, braved the taunts and threats of her New Orleans classmates and their parents?

The world we inhabit is hardly innocent, is it? I was born at the midpoint of a decade filled with expansive optimism and Cold War rumors. In the middle of a century that some historians argue was the most violent in terms of sheer millions of lives lost at the hands of oppressive governments. Our global reality remains scarred by trauma, violence, war, and genocidal urges. We inhabit a daily world where human beings love and reach out a hand or fail at love, and in the worst moments, in the worst way, with intent to tear down or push someone away. We turn our backs on the suffering, insisting on refuge in our entertainment-centric living spaces. Swords and pistols, like in the nursery ballad, symbolize more than playthings but harsh realities.

Sometimes human suffering seems to throw in our face arguments for, at best, a distant Being too busy to keep such things from happening—One who won't condescend to pay attention, One who will not "soil" himself with the stuff of earth. The temptation to picture the deity as coldly distant is an old one. Maybe this hesitancy, born of God's immensity, is in the New Testament itself: "It is [God] alone who has immortality and dwells in unapproachable light, whom no one has ever seen or can see."[3] And yet the early followers of Jesus also said the unseeable became visible. Christ is "the image of the invisible God," Paul said.[4]

What we see is more than a pleasant scene. The immortal took on our mortality. The incorruptible willingly suffered the corruption of decay and death that had entered the human race in the fall. The word for that revelation—and event—is *incarnation*: the making flesh—from which we get words like *carnal*—of God in Christ's very self. The Son of God was also a Son of humanity. One of us.

A God-bathed and God-permeated world, to use Dallas

Willard's phrase,[5] sparks awe, but what moves us to turn to God in trust that we will find mercy? A college student once said to me, "I think God is looking down on me with a bemused smile." For her, that was progress, an outgrowth of hanging out in our campus fellowship, an advance from simply an impressive God. And that is, to be sure, better than picturing a studied frown or glaring eye. But in the unfolding story of the Trinity we see God more than showing mild fondness. More like a fierce love and mercy. A depth of kindness that will not leave us stranded in our self-loathing or guilt. That will not leave us drifting on a forgotten globe in an aimless universe.

WHAT I LEARNED IN ALEXANDRIA

Some years ago, I went to Egypt to teach a weekend course at the Anglican School of Theology in Alexandria. My students, living in a land sometimes hostile to Christianity, had much to teach *me.* Being in Egypt, I chose to teach about one of the church's important figures from Alexandria: the revered, sometimes embattled, fourth-century bishop Athanasius. I had known how Athanasius had insisted, against the heretic Arius (AD 256–336), on a fully divine picture of Jesus.

While reading Athanasius's book *On the Incarnation* and giving it one more glance before a lecture, I realized that one of his analogies drew on the Alexandrian seacoast I had just walked along near my apartment. "Such and so many are the Savior's achievements that follow from his Incarnation," he wrote, "that to try to number them is like gazing at an open sea and trying to count the waves. One cannot see all the waves with one's eyes, for when one tries to do so those that are following on baffle one's senses."[6] What might the "great achievements" of the incarnation mean?

I felt humbled by the immensity of what I was about to share with the students. And I wonder how you might, as I did again this morning before the day began, consider the waves of God's goodness that "follow" from Jesus' coming.

The early church stressed that Jesus was not a semi-god or an almost-God. God and Jesus shared one substance, one nature. Look at Jesus and you look at the heart of God the Creator. The Christian claim resounds with conviction that God becomes profoundly present in Christ—not just standing nearby, hovering in the wings, not just out there, but right *here*, fully close, where we find ourselves on any given day. Now and always part of the world's reality.

We look on and see in the Son the fullest picture possible of the Father. "We have seen and testify that the Father has sent his Son to be the Savior of the world," promised an early Christian writer. "If anyone acknowledges that Jesus is the Son of God, God lives in them and they in God."[7]

This is where Jesus tells us something profound about the Trinity. We see him relating intimately with the Father in his earthly life. He turned to a God he called Abba, a childlike, affectionate name, as we've seen. And God responded, we see, with a remarkable statement: "And a voice came from heaven," Mark told us, saying, "You are my Son, whom I love; with you I am well pleased."[8] But not surprising, in that a son shares the very nature of the one who gave him life.

It is natural to turn to the *Son* for help, not just the Creator-Father, to find how we can be held amid our this-life fears and hopes. The old word *providence* refers to the belief that God stays involved in the affairs of people—even individuals, like you and me. In the Christian story he did it in a very down-to-earth way, taking up residence in our very earthy existence. Getting the dirt of earth under his fingernails. The world is marred by sin, to be sure, but nevertheless not beyond the reach of God's loving hand and attentive involvement.

Jesus is even called God's Word (capital *W*) in the Bible. To speak of *logos* or word in this sense meant a thought turned over and over, then crystallized and shared. We use words, after all, not just to communicate about concrete things like tables, rocks, cars, and loaves of bread, but also to suggest something about our experience of these things. Otherwise, there would be no true communication. Words in this sense communicate something of our deeper selves, our souls.

The Greeks took that further, suggesting that beyond words, behind everything, really, is a larger idea or force. This logos represented the soul of things. It represented the thought that held everything together—the universal mind behind what we see. The Bible was reaching out to pagans, in a way, to use a word they could latch on to.

The early Christians took this idea from Greek philosophy—*logos*, literally "word"—and applied it to Jesus. He was, they said, the source of all creation and the means by which God reveals himself to humanity. The Jews in John's audience would have had their own thoughts and feelings stirred up by this image of the Word. The Jews believed that if words have power, God's words have immense power. Psalm 33:6 tells us, for example, that "by the word of the LORD the heavens were made." God said, after all, in Genesis, at the creation of the world, "'Let there be light, and there was light.'" God said, "Let the land produce living creatures." God said, and it happened.[9]

But John goes further, much further, than either the Greeks or Jews. Never would the Greeks, in their wildest imaginations, have believed that this rational principle that holds together the universe could become enfleshed in a human life. Never would the ancient Hebrews dared think that God's Word would become human.

But now, said John, look at Jesus, because in him the Word becomes visible. "In the beginning was the Word," John wrote.[10] He didn't adopt everything the Greek philosophers meant by the word when he applied it to Jesus, but he *was* saying: Look—this is what your philosophers are talking about when they suggest that there is intelligence behind this great universe. Now, said John, turn your eyes and attention on Jesus, because in him the Word becomes visible. And Jesus is the Word made clear.

"And the Word became flesh and lived among us," John wrote, "and we have seen his glory . . . full of grace and truth."[11] This Word came as a life made tangible and real. "God with skin on," as one child put it. With pounds on. With a real body that enters full physical human life. One who comes to help, to enter our lives and the life of the world. God speaks through him to our deepest heartaches and hopes.

This picture shows what we most long to know, what Reynolds Price called "the sentence that [hu]mankind craves from stories—*The Maker of all things loves and wants me.*"[12]

The Word was made a person, one who can be watched and listened to, whose touch can be felt. To the question, "Anybody out there?" we see an answer that has to do with *right here.* Through a child. One who would grow up to use his hands in ordinary and extraordinary ways, because God took residence in a human body. Julie Canlis talked about the domestic simplicity of the incarnation: "When He comes to earth, God places Himself not in a palace but in a *family.*"[13] To come close to us, he was born in the kind of place an ordinary person would live.

THE TRINITY WEPT?

In many ways, the Trinity becomes clearer here: We see this God-made-present in some striking ways when we look at Jesus and his life. We see the depths of *humanness* to which the Trinity submitted. I think of one example, among many: Known widely as the shortest verse in the Bible, John 11:35 is also one of the most dramatic: "Jesus wept," it says. It's not the first time someone in the New Testament cries, nor is it the first time tears appear in John 11. But Jesus weeping at the death of his friend Lazarus, which is what prompted the tears, has deeper layers. The word, when probed a bit in the original language, conveys a sense of "bursting into tears." There's a sense that the grief was not measured or mild but visceral.

When Jesus raised Lazarus from death, it marked the final of the Gospel of John's seven "signs"—such as turning water into wine. But pastor and writer Abram Kielsmeier-Jones asked: "What if Jesus' *bursting into tears* is also a sign in John? It would be a sign of his humanity . . . a sign of his witness to grief and 'with-ness' with us. It would be a sign of his ability *to be moved*."[14] A sign that God—Father, Son, and Holy Spirit—sees and knows what we face, the worst and the best, the communing and the loss. And because they don't exist apart, they work together, inseparably. Was it not the Father, Son, and Spirit who stood right there when Jesus not only grieved but also brought his friend back to life? They never compartmentalize when it comes to drawing close, saving, and helping. When God shows up, it's the whole show.

JESUS: FULLY HUMAN, FULLY GOD

Christ came into our world, not watching from afar but stepping into our pain and brokenness. He entered a creation that had strayed far from what its Creator first intended. This was more than insight delivered at a distance. He *burst into tears*. When the world seems intimidating, when relationships seem ready to tank, we see just how little we are alone. He lived out a story of something more real-life, rooted in the actual earth. God was made *flesh*, to use the rough-edged language of the Bible, with its connotation of earthy functions and everyday materiality—sweat, excrement, and sore muscles. Some of us like the idea of a pleasant strolling teacher, perhaps with a dozen miracles thrown in, but essentially your garden-variety guru. Divine, but only partly. It was, to be sure, a temptation in the early church.

A teacher in an influential fourth-century congregation might lend support to that view. Arius argued that we cannot speak of Jesus as an eternal Son, as fully divine. There was a time when the Son did not exist, he claimed. Arius taught that Jesus was a mediator between God and humankind, but only divine-ish, not fully, gloriously God in human flesh. He said if we call Jesus God, as the New Testament does, it is only as a kind of courtesy. I think this view is more common in our churches now than we might think.

I suppose it may seem less complicated, less prone to the difficulties of saying Jesus was fully God and fully human. Arius and his followers said Jesus was in some way divine, but, as human, inescapably subordinate and inferior to God. By that logic, there was a time when God was *not* a Father, which would mean God had to change when it was Jesus' time to jump in. But no, the early Christians who prevailed said God *always* was a Father. Jesus, the second person of the Trinity, was no add-on. As they proclaimed Jesus as Lord, they said that he was *always* the Son. If he was simply a lesser deity, then he was not fully God, not the logos made flesh.

Another group in the early church, the Gnostics, went in the other direction, saying Jesus the divine one could not have been *human*. Gnosticism taught that Christ's coming was purely spiritual, airy. God, they said, would never—*could* never—mingle with human flesh and fleshly existence. Because the material-physical dimension was corrupt, it could not contain God's full presence. Redemption did not require incarnation, they said. God's visitation could not be bodily and real. Perhaps part of you finds this tempting: Overlay the whole story with a pleasant spiritual glow. A nice stopover for a heavenly guest, this mortal plane, free of the grit and hardship of real life.

But something big was at stake here. Something essential that could be lost. Jesus' life was not a mere shell or disguise, untouched by human limits. He grew up amid the resinous smells of cut wood, even an occasional splinter in his finger. His stomach growled. He was God, but God in the flesh.

And Jesus came for the most ordinary people you can imagine. The Gnostics thought he came for the mega-spiritual types who float above the rest of us, skip naps, and can't enjoy a good meal. But he didn't show up for holy elites. That's not the Jesus I see in the Gospels—the one who hung around tired, messy people who seem less cranky after a good night's sleep.

Jesus' life was not a mere shell or disguise, untouched by human limits. He grew up amid the resinous smells of cut wood, even an occasional splinter in his finger. His stomach growled. He was God, but God in the flesh.

This Jesus helps us when we venture into a world of surprises, horrors, and hapless moments—like Froggy, like my mother, like me, like any of us. The elements of God's good creation, made even more holy by his inhabiting them, become means of grace, ways to meet God. The physical is indispensable. Early Christians knew this—things like eating bread and drinking wine to remember Jesus were central to their worship. The bread and wine have taste and texture. Baptism uses real water. These sacraments are physical on purpose. They are ways Jesus keeps showing up when we gather for worship.

The New Testament writers and the early church stressed that in Jesus, by becoming one with humanity in real life, God made an irrevocable commitment to our everyday hassles and hopes. There is nothing so small in humanity that God cannot bring good to it, cannot come close to us in it. Nothing in life is too small for God to somehow speak through. Your life—your *human* life—matters to

God; its triumphs and disappointments are not off-limits from the divine life. God has already come to live where we live.

GOD IN REAL PLACES, REAL TIME

Some background underlines how important the divine-human reality was and how much it aligned God's covenant with the people. The incarnation had to do with both our making and our redeeming—in real time. From the first pages of the Old Testament onward, we hear little teaching not tied to actual events, little truth expounded without story, little exposition about God without actual happenings. God shows up in the people's history, becomes their story. We can use the same focus on Jesus' real, lived presence to look at the whole Bible—even the parts before he arrived. This helps us notice signs of the Trinity throughout the entire story.

Take, for instance, an early story in Genesis. Abraham entertained three heavenly visitors at the "oak of Mamre"—a *place*. Were they angels? Were they, as some in the Russian Orthodox tradition believe, the persons of the Trinity incognito?

Or there's the Exodus, Israel's miracle-accompanied release from bondage in Egypt. Was the Trinity somehow, a Christian might ask, involved, working out divine purposes? Might it not make sense to muse that the three *could* have been tending to such an important encounter in the people of God's story?

I think also of how early in Israel's history, when they were still trekking toward the promised land, each time the people camped for an extended period, a tent marked the place where God lived among them. A tent! They were wanderers then. Later it was a tabernacle—a grander affair. Much later, more permanently, as more of them settled into cities, the temple became the focal point. An actual place of real estate in Jerusalem became God's home, his special dwelling place in Israel. A place where you'd find God especially close.

For the first-century Jew, Jerusalem was the center of the earth and the temple was the holiest spot on earth. Spirituality met hard terrain. Faith had some geography. This was the place where God dwelt, where he was visibly present. That presence made the people delight in the chance to gather and meet God. "I was glad when they said to me, 'Let us go to the house of the Lord.'"[15] They expected nothing less than an encounter.

And the temple animal sacrifices? They seem like a holdover from more primitive religion. But think of the way the practice would have jogged, if not jolted, the senses with the blood and smoke and incense. In the sights and sounds and smells they encountered a living God. The people's guilt, which they felt so keenly in times of struggle, met remedy and relief in a visceral way—an animal's gutted insides spoke of intense realities. They took home sense impressions they could hold on to when they faced the day's challenges.

As scholar N. T. Wright said, for Israel the temple was the place where heaven and earth came together and God was visibly present.[16] It was not lost on Jesus' earliest followers that *he* was where so much of God's activity was going on. Healings were only a part of it. Jesus could still a frightening storm. People plagued by impossibly heavy burdens of guilt and not-measuring-up found forgiveness. Those cast to the sides of the roads and put on the margins of society were brought back in, given a place and a calling. Made brand-new.

But this time, while the temple mattered so much before, God was showing up in a living, breathing, caring person. He was the temple made ambulatory—able to move into places of deep need and fear. He met people wounded by others and made them whole again. Better than a building, he was a person of flesh like us, except for our sin, in every way. And Jesus was not alone in this. Where

Jesus went, the Spirit of Christ—the Spirit of God—would not idly be shunted off.

JESUS: A VULNERABLE GOD WITH US

This kind of reflection could seem like ancient history, unrelated to the daily stresses we face. But I have another take. It offers something to consider when existence seems to be in crash mode, or our own life events tumble in on us. The New Testament affirms that the world isn't a desolate wasteland beyond repair—not if the eternal God walked into it, not just to hand out mercy and hope, but to live in it himself.

Then, in the church's project to articulate what God did in Christ, Irenaeus, a bishop in France and one of the earliest teachers and thinkers, made clear how God entered the world, inhabiting human life and affirming its worth. He felt he had to battle, like Athanasius would, the false teachings of those who could not imagine how the vast God of the cosmos could become fully, wonderfully human.[17]

This conviction has centered believers ever since and all along. Christians have prayed for centuries, "You, Christ, . . . did not shun the Virgin's womb," the "Te Deum," an early Christian hymn, puts it.[18] No room can contain God, of course, not even a temple, but God entered a womb, wrote Natalie Carnes, "the smallest room anyone ever inhabits."[19]

So not only are we vulnerable due to our humanness, but God also chose to share that vulnerability. He knew that we could survive but not fully thrive on the fumes of human love. But in Christ we see someone who saw all that we face. In Christ we see a fuller immersion in our life, even in the shadowy moments, the times a sword and pistol crop up in a ballad sung to a child.

When we look long and longingly at Jesus' advent, we see more than a solitary arrival. Jesus was accompanied by God. *Was* God. The Trinity is part of that grand story, too, showing a compassion writ large in the incarnation—the making flesh of God, the becoming earthly of what is heavenly and triune, right where we live and struggle and grieve and rejoice.

JULIAN ON EXPEDITION

A medieval figure has helped me make sense of the kinds of realities hinted at in Froggy's questing. A kind of spiritual adventurer, Julian of Norwich went on an expedition, a hunt, not riding out into a wider world but retreating into an enclosed space not much larger than a jail cell. Living centuries after Augustine, she grappled with disease, bloodshed, turmoil, and the headstrong human heart of her medieval England. What she wrote had a groundedness, for all its lofty glimpses. All these years of dipping into her writings, and only lately have I found her a deep resource for my hopes to experience more of the Trinity as connection and communion.

She looked around for common objects to make her points, for one thing. Ordinary stuff. The things of home and hearth and yard. Azure-blue clothing, "a cloth shaken in the wind," or, she would say, "the profusion" of the shed blood of Jesus "like the drops of water which fall from the eaves after a heavy shower of rain." God once showed her "a hazelnut" to make a point about how he could cup a whole world with protective care. And what can more tenderly depict a caring God's love than a mother and child? Reaching for the daily to speak of the lofty, Julian of Norwich said, God "is our clothing that out of love enwraps us and enfolds us, embraces us and wholly encloses us, surrounding us for tender love, so that he can never leave us."[20] Sometimes the simplest, most ordinary parts of life convey ways to think of the vast God, the earthly pointing to the heavenly.

But it's more than just the imagery or the way she chose to write. It's also her warmth. Her sense of the fiery love of God and awareness of Christ's tender love for her, and what that means for ordinary people like you and me.

TO GO OR NOT TO GO

I was traveling and faced a decision about Julian. This was the same trip in which I visited with Rowan Williams in his study, chatting about the Trinity and the relatedness at the heart of the world.

I was on sabbatical from my ministry work at a busy cathedral. Looking back, I'm doubly grateful—it was just months before COVID arrived to shut down most travel. I had a week in England, part of my almost three months of rest and study and renewal. Cambridge, my base for several days, had lots of charm—quaint streets, bookstores, choral evensongs, remarkable conversations, and a coffee shop with perhaps the best oat-milk latte I've ever had.

Norwich had also caught my attention—the city of Julian, the first woman who can be identified as writing in the English language. Years before, I had read Julian of Norwich's *Revelations of Divine Love*, including her oft-quoted line, "All shall be well . . . and all manner of thing shall be well."[21] Pleasant enough. And while over the years I dipped into her dense writing, I wouldn't say she was one of my desert-island authors.

Besides, one of my seminary professors once downplayed her significance. I think he saw her as someone attractive to pop culture but not deep. Her "All shall be well" might have inclined him to dismiss her as a theological lightweight.

Compounding my indecision, Norwich was an hour-and-a-half

train ride from my base in Cambridge. The trip to a city in England's east, replete with the country's must-see Gothic cathedral and medieval cobblestone streets, would take the better part of a day. I debated. I almost didn't go.

But that early visit in Cambridge in Rowan's office and study again made a difference. I realized I could share with him my internal debate. And with a bemused smile he weighed in.

"You should go!" he said.

Who was I to question the spiritual direction of an archbishop?

So the next day I hopped on a train. I did indeed alight at Norwich Cathedral, which had its own impressive tourist glories. But I recall most vividly Julian's reconstructed cell attached to a little stone church. The entire space where she lived was smaller than a suburban bedroom, and I absorbed some of the atmosphere of the shrine, its bare simplicity, its holy quiet. "Here dwelt Mother Julian," said a sentence chiseled into a stone portion of the wall. There she lived at least twenty years, much of the time praying and writing sublime prose about God's love. There she lived, *never leaving.*

She wasn't a nun, but her lifelong vow of enclosure was even more dramatic than that of cloistered convents. More solitary. Her tiny room was called an anchor-hold, from a Greek word meaning retire or withdraw. She was called an anchoress.

And there in that cell she reflected intently on an intense experience of God's presence and heightened awareness that took place over a few days in May 1373. She actually asked to suffer if it would draw her closer to God. It's not the kind of praying we are used to these days, when we more likely cry out for *relief* from suffering. As it turned out, illness came—almost fatally. But here I began to see how she grappled with faith in a loving God while squaring with a world that hosted the worst things imaginable.

We don't know a lot about her life before she received the visions she called "showings." She had already been a faithful churchgoer—likely *daily* attendance at Mass—and doer of charitable acts, but she longed for a more profound experience of God's love in Christ, especially to experience Christ's suffering as he approached the cross. Was she a widow? Possibly. The plague—the Black Death—killed off as much as half the population of the river port town, and perhaps that included a husband—her own. And even felled a son? We don't know.

As I learned more, I came to see that for all her hopeful words about all being well, she lived in times more distressed than our own. Julian would have been seven years old or so when the plague hit hard. Medieval historian Barbara Tuchman called it the "most lethal disaster of recorded history."[22] Some peg the Black Death as one of history's worst catastrophes. It's estimated that a third of England's population died.

And that's to say nothing of the other stresses: war, oppressive taxes, robbery, bad government, political revolt, schism in the church, and the bloodshed of the Hundred Years' War. Oh, and famine. Her cell sat on the main thoroughfare through the bustling city, close to the docks and the red-light district—a clear sight line to the tempted, the suffering, and the poor.

When a local peasant leader that she might have known, Geoffrey Litster, led a peasants' rebellion, he was executed near Julian's cell, which was affixed to the church. Might she have heard the commotion and cries through her window?

With my visit to her cell fresh in my mind, I came to see Julian as a patron saint of the pandemic that would soon descend on our lives, just a year after my visit, upending seemingly everything. I would now enlarge that description of her potential role: a patron saint for any time of large-scale chaos. A guide for anxious times. A voice from the past relevant for the personal struggle or the chaos of our inner worlds. Not just catchy quotes. But profound connecting points that give her radiant faith such resonance with our own times—what has drawn me back again to her dense and somehow also shining prose.

She gives me words that help me realize I am not only made but also *held*. I see how someone like her can help me make sense of my life and these hard prospects in light of the Trinity. Her take on God in the one book she wrote, abounding in kindness and grace, a manuscript that's managed to survive all these hundreds of years since, steeps its prose in the Father at the heart of the Trinity's communion.

She reached deep into her own experience to enrich her church's traditional language with imagery of both a father's and a mother's kindness, along with a dawning certainty about joys possible for a child of God. Might we learn something here about how, amid the world's hurts and harms, there is companioning—a God who in Christ drew close and became subject to the hardships that visit human life in every age?

And then I think of this: Did her reclusive life give her more in common with us, we who feel as alone and rudderless as ever? Might not our own isolation, while serious and not to be overspiritualized, be seen as an invitation to experience more of God's drawing close? Might not Julian's retreat from society have made her more prone to consider the intensely relational aspects of God's nature? In her seclusion, she clearly grew in communion and friendship with the divine.

She spoke, after all, of a sublime love of fatherly, heavenly proportions, along with a motherly side to the Eternal's tender care for us. "I saw," she wrote in her *Revelations of Divine Love*, "that God rejoices that he is our father, God rejoices that he is our mother, and God rejoices that he is our true spouse, and our soul is his beloved wife. And Christ rejoices that he is our brother, and Jesus rejoices that he is our Savior."[23] She knew spiritual realities stretched over us. Or ran under us like a subterranean stream. And if rooted in the good earth, through Jesus' incarnation, God was not and could not be limited by the world. "For our soul is so especially loved by him who is highest that it surpasses the knowledge of all created beings—that is to say, there is no being made who can know how much and how sweetly and how tenderly our maker loves us."[24]

We might revere a God who displays his infinite majesty in power. But for One who figures out how to get through to us, to touch our hearts, cry with us? I love how Athanasius put it: "Some may ask," he wrote, "why did [God] not manifest himself by means of other and nobler parts of creation such as sun or moon or stars or fire or air, instead of mere man? The answer is this: The Lord did not come to make a display. He came to heal and to teach suffering people."[25]

That's what we long for: Someone who walks with us, who sits with us in our grief. Like a mother rocking a child. It's simple. Simple and wonderful.

MEETING CHRIST FOR MYSELF

I think of a time when what I'm describing became clearer. How I found life opening to a God who met me. As a young person, I had an encounter—long before I knew about Augustine or Julian—that would help temper the power of my parents' rejection. The faith that mattered so much to my mother also gave me strength, in ways she never expected, especially when her only goal seemed to be to keep me close.

It happened like this: Like nearly everyone else in my straight-lined blocks of flat ranch homes in my Southern California suburb in 1968, I faced the normal stresses of adolescence at school. Would I fit in? I was lanky—"Jones Bones" some of my classmates called me. A growth spurt left my cotton pants short around the ankles.

"Waiting for a flood?" jibed another, more or less good-naturedly. My dad worked a short drive away building filters for the engines of rockets that would take astronauts in fiery liftoffs to the moon. I thought mostly about everyday matters—friends, a girl I liked but around whom I felt awkward, classes at Columbus Junior High.

But I was about to discover something more significant than belonging among my friends. The childhood God to whom I had lobbed prayers, the Being I had vaguely reverenced on Sundays—could that Being dwell not just up there or out there but, well, *here*?

Earlier as a child I had routinely sung in Sunday school classes, "Jesus loves me, this I know." A tale not as dramatic as Froggy's, certainly more religious. But I don't recall that it inspired much.

One day at lunch at Columbus Junior High, my best friend Donald Lopez and I were joined by a classmate named Stan. Don, whose parents were a Polish Jew and a Mexican Catholic, was exploring his identity and faith. He even signed my yearbook as "the Jewish Chicano." Stan, known for being the best-dressed in school, had recently gotten involved in a lively church in California and spoke about it openly.

Church and Sunday school hadn't given me much personal connection to my faith. I doubt if I had anything but distant glimmers of the deep, relational love shown in the Trinity. I hadn't thought much about a heavenly Father, nor, for that matter, how a mother's care might reflect the tenderness of God in Christ.

At one point Stan asked my friend Don, "Have you ever read the Bible?" I don't remember what Don said, but I will never forget the answer that began to form in me: No, I *hadn't*.

I went home and began making my way through the Gospels. I found myself pulled into the intimate stories of a Jesus who blessed children with a gentle gesture, who healed with a touch, who looked at people with compassion and even wept, who trudged to the cross.

And almost immediately I became aware of a kind Presence. I

had already believed things about God, of course, but now I began to sense—at times with a leap in my heart—that here and now Christ had come close.

If before I had intimations of the bigness of God, the vastness of a universe that left me in awe, here, in the Gospels, I found glimpses of Jesus' face of compassion. I experienced something compelling: God was willing to take up residence not only centuries ago but also as a living Presence in my own life. It came with a bit of awe, a recognition that Someone can care as fiercely and fervently as any mother or father and—good news—more.

And there would be yet more—a deepening as I continued to explore this communion now possible. I'd come to find that at the Trinity's hot core, something could be glimpsed that I'd almost overlooked: a gut-punch climax—a seeming tragedy, by all appearance a dreary disappointment, along with an astonishing conclusion. Not only the Son's birth, but also the way forward for our rebirth. Not just the Son crying on the cross to his Father, *Why have you forsaken me?* but an astonishing repair of the cataclysm of humanity's breakage, to which we now turn our attention.

SIX

WILL LOVE FIND AND MEND ME?

But quick-eyed Love, observing me grow slack
From my first entrance in,
Drew nearer to me, sweetly questioning,
If I lacked any thing.
—George Herbert

Could a body broken and blood spilled two thousand years ago restore my own damaged life?
—Frederica Mathewes-Green

SOMEONE IN THE PARK WAS SHOUTING. AS JILL AND I kept walking, the yelling got louder.

Newly married, we were strolling along the palisades of Santa Monica overlooking the ocean. The day was awash with Southern California sunshine.

"What are you doing here?" the voice shrieked.

I realized with a start that it came from a woman looking at us—glaring at me. The cry had the sense of *Why in the world are you here? Why?* Her graying hair was mussed by the breezes off the ocean, more or less held in place by a scarf she'd tied on.

She had a bag sitting by her on the park bench. Later Jill would tell me that when she heard the shouting and first looked, she thought she was seeing a homeless person, a bag lady. Her cry was not a philosophical question, nor a friendly one. It carried notes of betrayal and hurt, an anguish I finally realized was directed at me.

"Do you know her?" Jill asked.

"It's my *mom*," I said.

"Just wait here," I told Jill, "and I'll go talk to her." Jill later told me my face had gone ashen.

I don't remember what we said when I went up. Of course, if it had been anyone else, I could have tried to answer the question about why I was there with a simple fact: "Well, I'm walking with my new wife, and I wanted to show Jill where I had long come to run or think or pray." I had jogged the palisade paths many times, palms swaying in the sea-salt-cleansed air, the laurel bushes pungent on the cliffside below.

I would have said I had come back home just before my last year of graduate theological school.

But the question my mother yelled didn't seem to ask or wonder as much as wound. Or erupt from a gathered pain. It came from someone I had known as a fount of warmth, someone I would go to when hurting—not someone who inflicted hurt. But she could not stand that I had married against her wishes.

I turned and rejoined Jill, and we went back to our Toyota. As we sat there with hands clasped, I sank my head on the unpadded steering wheel and sobbed. We both did.

Many years later, I offered a draft of my story at a writer's workshop, and the leader, a seasoned author, found it puzzling; it was so extreme. "Why would your mother be so hostile?"

I can speculate about the ways Mom had so self-isolated, so relentlessly neglected friends and family that she couldn't bear the thought of giving me up to another. Maybe I was witnessing the earliest signs of dementia that would later come into full view. And as I'm often asked, yes, there was reconciliation eventually.

But the reality of our human brokenness is that those we love the most sometimes reject us in puzzling, even extreme ways.

Whatever the specific pain—the loss, rejection, or betrayal—people shove us away. We feel steered—maybe pushed—into a dark place. Early in my journey to maturity, I had to confront our human experience of absence: of loved ones we lose, of love we long for but never experience fully, of relationships we ourselves bungle and sabotage. We often feel alone, without full and rich connections. That's our world. Sometimes, too, that's our experience of a God we seem to have lost contact with.

The narrative of the Christian faith became compelling to me in an unfolding way, in an account found in classical beliefs that still seem contemporary. As an adolescent I met the second person of the Trinity while reading the accounts of his life, but also in confronting his death. I saw how God's storyline recognizes that our deepest hardships revolve around our not being loved. Our nagging anxieties grow out of fears of not being accepted by someone whose love we counted on to be steadfast and sure. The lights of the home we loved go dark. The front door swings shut with us on the outside. Maybe we are subjected to public shaming, embarrassed beyond belief, made fun of for not only what we did or didn't do but for who and what we are.

God's storyline recognizes that our deepest hardships revolve around our not being loved.

Strahan Coleman told of a friend "going through a bad break-up," who shared "that the loneliness made him feel like a 'cosmic orphan.'"[1] It can feel like God's gone away or just got too busy to notice—or care.

We long to know that we can expect something different from God—that we can experience a warming love, holding us as a mother at her loving best would hold us, as a mercy-filled father would welcome us. As my friend Sarah Condon put it, "I speak to myself more gently than I ever thought I would."[2] And, she said, it was because of the tenderness of God's voice. Because of the kindness of Christ.

But the response to our questions has to be more than facile or glib. More like something proven than promised. Lived out, not just set on a calligraphy plaque. They feel more like hard questions lived on the edge of hope or endurance. As I write about the love I find in communing with God—with the Trinity, Father, Son, Holy Spirit—I find myself more intrigued than ever with the drama of the cross.

How might Christ, the second person of the Trinity incarnate, the son of Mary, both divine and a very human person, somehow square with the serene picture we get of the persons of the Trinity in kind communion? In what ways can the crucifixion, for all its offense and shame, make the Trinity more real?

When I began asking that question, I wasn't prepared for the onslaught of detail from the biblical story. What I found moved me to awe and gratitude.

For as the drama that I am coming to see in the Trinity continues to unfold, I see how the story does not stop with a Father-Creator, or even a Savior-Son. Also at work in bringing us nearer to God and one another is John Donne's "three-personed God."[3] Even in the tortuous parts of the story, the gritty parts where we'd maybe rather avert our eyes, when we witness the suffering, seemingly final end of the Son of God's sojourn on earth—here, too, something essential gets fleshed out. He walked our dusty roads and detours and dead ends knowing his life moved toward a dismal dark outcome, willingly walking into a human-inflicted distancing and forsakenness that could make the hairs on our necks stand on end, if we had not heard the story so often. And yet whatever the strain and sorrows, there was no severing of communion. The Trinity was not "broken" or the Son's trust shattered. That's the backdrop of assurance on which to ground the harrowing details of the story that follows.

WHEN LOVE MEETS REJECTION

I like what Philip Yancey said about most biographies: how few will, when you think about it, devote more than 10 percent of their pages to the subject's death—including biographies of men like Martin Luther King Jr. and Mahatma Gandhi "who died violent and politically significant deaths." The Gospels, however, "devote nearly a third of their length to the climactic [and chaotic] last week of Jesus' life. Matthew, Mark, Luke, and John," he wrote, "saw the death of Jesus as the center for understanding his life, and the cornerstone of our faith."[4]

The incarnation pretty well settles that the Son of God does not live solely in heavenly bliss, floating in a celestial stratosphere. He descended to join with humanity, to know its daily hardships and the worst of its horrors, which is where this chapter turns its attention. He experienced the metallic taste of blood, forehead skin sagging under the crown of thorny spikes, and even worse, the despair of being despised and abandoned—a series of heartbreaking scenes.

When Christians argue that Christ was fully divine and fully human, what do we make of Christ's lonely journey through rejection, mockery, and unjust sentencing? Where was God in that? Do we see an unfortunate but random death, or a toxic heavenly Father, as some portray?

These harsher turns in the story of the Son of God's suffering and death ring true to life's hardness and wreckage. I think of the battering ram of our own relational disasters and disappointments. Here instead, we see a God of costly kinship and self-sacrificial kindness, a Father whose love weathers the worst that human life can inflict, a Son who undergoes rejection at the hands of humanity, and even then communed with, prayed to, his Father. If death did not sever the communal life of the Trinity, then what we see in this picture of God possesses great power to assure. The Holy Spirit had not skipped out of town. Jesus continues to turn to the Father, trustingly. The *Father* did not reject the Son.

At the same time, the drama shines out. God does not clutch the Son, the Son does not cling to his "Godness," the Holy Spirit still moves as from all eternity. In Philippians 2, we glimpse a picture of Jesus,

> *Who, being in very nature God,*
>   *did not consider equality with God*
> *something to be used to his own advantage;*
> *rather, he made himself nothing*
>   *by taking the very nature of a servant,*
>   *being made in human likeness.*
> *And being found in appearance as a man,*
>   *he humbled himself*
>   *by becoming obedient to death—*
> *even death on a cross!*[5]

Humbled himself indeed. In Jesus' blood-stained robe and raw flesh is a panorama grittier, more real-life than the Sunday school flannel boards and sunshiny pictures suggest. We might revere a God who in power displays his infinite majesty, or warm at the thought of one who comes in the loveliness of gentleness. But for there to be love, it takes One who figures out how to get through to us, to share our suffering, to brave what makes us most afraid, most abject. Most desperate. The gospel, as E. Lily Yu wrote, is "the story of how God loved the world enough to enter into its sufferings and sorrows and humiliations and die in pain and disgrace on our behalf, so that we might become His children, if we choose, and return His love."[6]

The story comes to a point in a question: What might it mean if Jesus joined with us in all the sorrows of human brokenness—even faced searing rejection by his own people, even for a moment wondered if he'd been abandoned by all his friends, even God? What if he faced what we will never experience but once—death—and came out on the other side?

Such questions matter because of how much help we need. We long for reclamation from the wreckage of human life. We need a rescue operation.

A GIFT, NOT A REWARD

In our achievement-oriented culture, in our accomplishment-driven world, we might be tempted to think a relationship with God is something we wrest from effort. It's up to us to effect reconciliation, if there's a breach. It's something we wrangle or finagle. A status or a state to achieve, not receive. Mercy, then, comes as a reward, not a gift. Something earned, not given. A muscular effort that leaves us self-congratulatory afterward. But there has to be more.

Sin is more than a human hobby; it has more of a grip on us.

"Deliverance and atonement must come from outside our sphere of influence," wrote Fleming Rutledge, "for we are powerless to save ourselves from Sin's sphere of power."[7] We feel bound, sometimes without even understanding the draw and pull of wrong, temptation, evil. We feel stuck. We don't just need more willpower or an inspirational speech.

I've heard Fleming preach in person, and her urgent, authoritative voice only underlines the seriousness of the message. She knows she comes to congregations often with a hard, sobering word. Her books don't quite fit the maximize-your-self-potential mood of our times. But she feels anything less is false, facile. Here is one reason I find the Trinity, a belief that some people have given up on as too lofty or confusing, so compelling. And real. Its storyline recognizes that we need more than a little pat on the shoulder. More than calls to live our "best life now." Self-reliance cannot repair the wrecked scenes of estrangement.

And Fleming knew she was not alone in history. Anselm of Canterbury, the medieval thinker, reminds us that we are not able to fix ourselves. As Anselm said, "Consider that the human race, that work of God's so very precious, was wholly ruined . . . and moreover, that this purpose could not be carried into effect unless the human race were delivered by their Creator himself."[8] Ruined? *Really*? Sometimes when tempted to think that portrayal is too stringent, too strong, we might want to pick up a newsfeed and see measureless cruelty. And not just by people "over there," but down the street, in the neighborhood—and even in a home we know.

Someone once shared her story with a small group at a church I served. Growing up, she recounted, "I was active in my Methodist church and the youth group. I thought I would keep rules and try to be a good church girl, and then God would help me with my life. He would be there to smooth the edges and take care of me."

But then a campus group in college brought her in contact with people who had a more full-bodied faith. She noticed how they saw God as more than a vaguely benevolent presence she could count on to bless her self-involved plans. And while in many ways her new college friends were ahead of her in piety and commitment, they seemed at the same time more conscious of sin in their lives. They had a more profound sense of humility. They spoke of Christ's forgiveness in a way that seemed deeper and more intense.

She told us, "I had been tempted before to simply say, 'No one's perfect and Christ died for sins,' but I didn't really see what Christ died for. But I looked deeper and saw my own heart, its slothfulness, selfishness, its capacity for vengefulness and jealousy. I learned to call sin *sin* and then look to Christ for mercy. And my faith came alive."

We may feel a sense of unrighteousness and shame, to be sure, in such a recognition, but simultaneously see an offer of the way through it. It's not like God says an easy, empty "Okay" to leave us where we were. We see the real possibility—even the promise—that our distance and division can be healed, no matter the cosmic cost. Before our eyes, as we trace the life of the Trinity touching down at the cross, we see more than kindly care—we see hope and extravagant mercy. We're talking about something hard-won. Not to leave us sitting in misery or melancholy but to move us to reverence and openness.

REJECTION AND RIDICULE

When we look at Jesus' last days, we may wrongly focus only on the physical pangs, the bodily pain. And to be clear, those were gruesome enough. Preachers aiming for effect can seem to relish the drama of the blood and lung-aching torture. But it's the rejection and ridicule that especially interested the New Testament writers. They said a lot about the humiliation of Jesus' execution. They stressed how he strode into the crisis and, out of pure love and with immense courage for us, endured shame.

Yes, excruciating pain is assumed. But betrayal by one of his followers, then denial by Peter, one of his most stalwart supporters—that's the story just getting warmed up. The religious leaders, furious, demanded his death—rejection by those in power. Even Jesus' trial, leading up to his death, involved taunting. The portrait we get of the Roman governor Pontius Pilate, representing the government and carrying out the trial, has undertones of sarcasm.

He paraded Jesus before the crowd with his crown of thorns and purple robe, ridiculing Jesus' claim to be a king. The flogging not only reduced him to a back of shredded flesh but also left him a seemingly passive victim. Pilate had somebody write an inscription and put it on the cross, written in Hebrew, Latin, and Greek, "The King of the Jews"—mocking him again. The soldiers taunted him, saying, "Hail, King of the Jews"—pure derision.

Is it possible that some there, calling for his death, had been at the temple when Jesus was twelve, impressed by his wisdom? Turning on him now with a sneer? Certainly, some in the crowd had witnessed his healings, heard his teaching, and greeted his Palm Sunday entrance. Did they now turn and despise him, shout for his death?

Crucifixion itself was designed to embarrass and shame the accused—the accursed—in a very public way. The word *cursed* appears more than once in Scripture. Some suggest that other deaths may be more prolonged than the three hours of Jesus hanging on the cross in the Gospel accounts. Human cruelty is so unfathomable that a person could suffer longer. But crucifixion was uniquely, diabolically ingenious for its combination of pain and shame.

The Romans placed the crosses of the crucified as roadside

advertisements of the grossness of the sorry process. They invited travelers to heap abject scorn. It was as if to say: "These miserable beings that you see before you," wrote Fleming Rutledge, "are not of the same species as the rest of us. The purpose of pinning the victim up like insects was to invite the gratuitous abuse of the passersby. Those in the crowd understood that their role was to increase, by jeering and mocking, the degradation of those who had been thus designated unfit to live."[9]

All this, of course, confronts the thoughtful believer with something potentially upsetting. The story of Jesus, particularly as read and portrayed in many churches' Holy Week worship services, puts before us something jarring and sobering. We may try to pass quickly over the sheer sadness. I understand that impulse. Each year holds for many of us a somber season called Lent, beginning with Ash Wednesday and culminating in Holy Week, Good Friday, and a sad Saturday. It's tempting to want to quickly get through it.

There's glory in the message we tell on Good Friday, what could be called Black Friday, but also a bit of the gory: Often the service for the day includes a recital of all the story's gruesome details. The cross, when we look hard, was not only dramatic but traumatic. So compelling that it tastes like sand in the mouth when you're at the beach, gravelly instead of smooth like water or silk.

This is not cosmic child abuse, but God willingly submitting to the suffering that true love entails. Jesus died alone on the cross, you could say, looking at the accounts, but there never occurs to me, reading them, any sense that the Son suffered neglect from an angry Father while a distant, disinterested Holy Spirit stood off gazing into the distance. Rather, the whole array of the Trinity's loving communion allowed for this disruption, willingly participating in the horrors. Willingly doing all that could be done to save us from our sins and from death itself.

THE CREATOR GETS DRASTIC

This portrait is remarkable. We are used to speaking of majesty in the Father. We see authority in the Son that makes us stand up straight; we see in him light from light, true God from true God, as the creed says. And the Spirit impresses with its power and prescience and movement. But the gift of a child in Bethlehem, with all the angelic fanfare, led also to the grit of a death in Jerusalem. That was the twist.

This turn surprised even Jesus' first followers, despite how he tried to warn them. He was clear in foreshadowing what would happen. But when it actually unfolded, Jesus' disciples caved in emotionally. They just *left*—deserted him—before he cried out on the cross with the so-called seven last words—words that exhibit a crushing agony.

In Christ, the Creator acts drastically, offering to us what we could never win, create, or accomplish. And the cross points to this more emotionally costly way. "It costs God nothing, so far as we know," wrote C. S. Lewis, "to create nice things; but to convert rebellious wills cost Him crucifixion."[10]

"Christ also suffered once for sins," Peter told us, "the righteous for the unrighteous, to bring you to God."[11] And when Peter said, "the righteous for the unrighteous," and that he did it "once," he meant that his death was sufficient, final, and adequate. Jesus felt the effects of our spiritual death, bore our suffering, took on our sin. He submitted to the rejection implicit and rampant in a fallen world.

That's not winking indulgence. It's God taking on the estrangement we experience, so determined is he to let nothing keep us apart. It's God declaring that nothing—not even our worst selves—will separate us from his love in Christ. As the Easter vigil prayer in *The Book of Common Prayer* reads: "How wonderful and beyond our knowing is your mercy and loving-kindness to us, that to redeem a slave [as in you and me], you gave us a son."[12]

LOVE WILLING TO SUFFER

But there is also some debate in all this. I am moved by what theologian Jürgen Moltmann called the "suffering of love."[13] This is where the cross moves us and stirs in us something more profound than sunshiny spirituality. Here we watch the Son willingly submit, along with the joys, to the worst parts of human life. *Willingly* is the operative word. Moltmann went too far in suggesting that God the Father or God as Trinity somehow is *subject* to suffering. Not when we maintain that God is, to use a couple of old words, *immutable* (too mighty to change) or *impassible* (too steadfast to be at the mercy of any feeling or experience).

And God, unlike us, is free from the unbridled influence emotions can have over us. As we sometimes say, emotions make us act in ways we have no control over. That picture cannot come close to applying to God. Here we see a mercy that is not manipulated or influenced; it's too overflowingly abundant for that. Too freely offered. God is not persuaded by any faux-martyr voice or attempts at manipulated maudlin excess. God is not obligated in that way, nor prone to the changing seasons of any feelings.

God is, in more than one sense, above all that causes us hurt and fear. Yet *pastorally*, when Moltmann wrote *The Crucified God*, something in my soul stood at attention. God hasn't absconded, hasn't left the scene, is somehow still present, but the cosmos hurts, groans. The Trinity is not broken, and even when Jesus cried, "My God, my God, why have you forsaken me?"[14] he was addressing his aching voice to God, *his* God.

Psalm 22, from which this pained phrase comes, declares God to be ever "the Holy One." And God's people, even in their extremity, said to God, "In you [O God] they trusted and were not put to shame."[15] I see here a holy tension, for it is also true that Jesus, Son of God, *suffered*. And as the creed says, as if to make it all the more situated in reality, in history, "suffered under Pontius Pilate."[16]

To love is not only to feel ecstatic joy. It also means mourning when the beloved turns away, dishes out rejection, or walks off, shrugging shoulders as if to care less. Does the whole Trinity not feel moved when humankind crucifies One sent to do good and be God in our midst? And for that we have precedent in Scripture: God the Father himself seemed to ache. Jesus, in his life, wept. The Holy Spirit grieved. But the whole scene at the cross, for its lacerating reality, is for our good. This moment is not cringing submission to forces of fate or hate, but rather generosity beyond the ability of our telling. It hurts in some ways to witness it, but does it not melt our resistance?

Poet and priest John Donne's poem "Good Friday, 1613. Riding Westward" speaks of "the spectacle of too much weight"—the almost unbearable sight of Christ's cross. Donne, as the character in the poem riding away from the scene of the crucifixion, does not, like Froggy, carry sword and pistol against the world he faces. Instead, he takes the journey with awe at God's love.[17]

NO CUDGEL TO WIELD

Early on, what I read or heard in church circles pointed me to the oft-quoted verse, John 3:16, that said that God so loved the world that he gave his only Son. Somehow that scene so formed my view of God—that picture of a generous, sacrificially loving God—that I mostly floated above the judgment-tinged, finger-pointing, pulpit-pounding rhetoric and brimstone threats that some have suffered under. I mean those who have fallen under that strain of harsh theology that left some folks' self-regard in tatters. Whatever was actually mouthed, some people recount bearing a portrayal of a God who harms and wields a cudgel—an avenger.

The rejection I experienced from my folks keeps me coming back to Jesus' betrayal and forsakenness, in a way that offers comfort. By the light of this portrait of self-sacrificial courage, suffering is not a problem to be solved but, astonishingly, an aspect of existence God sees and knows. Pain is somehow intertwined, in ways I can't begin to fathom, with God's Trinitarian communing.

"It is indeed," said Thomas Torrance, "God's threefold giving of himself to us as Father, Son, and Holy Spirit that is our salvation."[18] Yes, Jesus cried out in forsakenness, but that was not the last word. In the passage from 1 Peter I mentioned earlier, where we read, "Christ also suffered once for sins, the righteous for the unrighteous," we also read, "he was put to death in the body but made alive in the Spirit."[19] The Spirit participates in redressing the whole drama of death and life.

The Three are, to use a ten-dollar word, *consubstantial.* Early Christians employed this word to express that the three shared one substance. Yes, there are personal dimensions, a threeness within the unity, and yet Father, Son, and Spirit share the same essence. There is enough of whatever it was that made God *God* to go around, to be in common among the Persons.[20] Whatever we say about the forsakenness on display, the saving work was triune. We see something here gloriously part of God's whole nature.

Julian of Norwich knew this. She asked her priest to place a crucifix in her full view when she thought she was dying. There was no prettiness to the blood her eyelids opened to. If God not only loves, but *is* love, she knew, then he will not shrink from the aching inherent in the world. God acts for restoration. Hung on the cross beams, Christ cries out while going across and mending the rift between us and our Maker. The Spirit tends those scattered from the foot of the cross, even then, not neglecting them or retreating from the continued work the Spirit will accomplish. And the Spirit soon will remind them that more would be on the way, that death could not be the universe's final answer to such loss.

Now, with the Trinity as a dramatic backdrop, I see better the communion of the Persons, the mutual love and self-giving among the godhead, in ways that help me know how un-alone I am. Even God involves his own self and personhood. My own experiences of estrangement do not lie outside of the scope of God's work. Christ's rejection by humankind is tied up with our moments of rejection. Our losses become gathered up in a life, death, and resurrection that withstands the worst we can experience.

At a clergy retreat at a church camp in a late winter in the sandy riverside woodlands of South Carolina, the leader, a woman who was part of a religious order, had us read a few of the stories in the Gospels about Jesus' last days—his worrisome progress toward suffering and death, exactly what he would meet in Jerusalem. Just before, he had lamented, "Jerusalem, Jerusalem, you who kill the prophets and stone those sent to you, how often I have longed to gather your children together, as a hen gathers her chicks under her wings."[21] It didn't take much effort to see the pathos building. "Now before the festival of the Passover," John recounted, she reminded us, "Jesus knew that his hour had come to depart from this world and go to the Father."[22]

I want to underline that little word: *to.* As she spoke, I remembered something about that tiny word that might seem insignificant but carries a larger meaning. It is sometimes translated "with," as in the prologue to John's Gospel: "The Word was *with* God, and the Word was God," John declared.[23] But even more the word *with* means "toward." "Far from being a static relationship," Michael Casey, one keen writer, noted, Jesus the embodied "Word is constantly pressing closer and closer to the Father, eternally penetrating more deeply into the heart of God."[24] In this, Jesus is joined to God and God to Jesus through the Holy Spirit.

With—not just in proximity but in intimate relationship. *To*—moving toward the intimacy he had and will always have. He was not just *with* God in the beginning, then, but at the end of earthly life. Jesus moved *toward* an end that included his Father's eternal love. His death was not just leaving but also heading back toward another home, to his Father. I see another hint or even glimpse of the Trinity: not just plodding ahead but determined steps of someone loved moving toward Someone loved.

This death was deeply different, reversing the usual way of the world. Distance, forsakenness, and *God*-forsakenness lose their estranging power. God will not allow any breakdown in fellowship with us and him to be the last word. He comes among us in and through a Son's sacrifice, restoring what has been broken and devastated. Doing for us what we could not do for ourselves—*saving* us. That is what a word like *atonement* begins to mean.

We long for connection like that. Rejection or being slighted—made *slight,* made *little*—takes so many forms in the world. I've put a spotlight on some. I think of yet others.

People without homes often live away from the usual places of rest, connection, and care. Those who work with the homeless say what hurts them most isn't someone taking a pass on giving financial help—it's being ignored, made invisible. Passersby avoid eye contact, refuse a simple nod, and act as if they don't exist at all.

Other forms of rejection are cruel too. Recently I discovered a website that documents postcards of lynchings in earlier times in America, most of the victims Black. The scenes, printed for mass distribution, depict wrenching brutality and marks of torture leading up to the hangings. I'm struck by the nonchalance of the perpetrators in the snapped scenes and the fact that the photographs, some capturing a carnival-like atmosphere with children present, became postcard "souvenirs"—a grotesque testimony to the way humans can grossly dehumanize one another. Sometimes we are, aren't we, taken aback by a group or tribe's calculated attempt to squelch the dignity and humanity of others?

My discovery of these atrocities coincided with a memory from an earlier season of Lent.

It was a sermon I heard about the cross of Christ. The preacher reminded those of us present how Jesus' crucifixion didn't just mean excruciating, mind-exploding pain and shame but also this: The execution method was perversely designed to deny and erase the memory of the accused. The method of killing was designed to leave something repugnant as the last image of the crucified or hung, especially for those who loved, honored, or followed the person. So distasteful was it that the memory would drive you to want to deep-six it. The act reduced the other to nothingness, to nonpersonness. It aimed to obliterate not only the victim's worth but any lingering memory of the person, pushing them to the edges of oblivion.

But something else, wildly different, happened with Jesus' crucifixion. It is true that at first his agony and squeezed-out, stolen breath reduced his friends to sorrowing disbelief. But only for a time.

And if death, wrote Rowan Williams, "is normally a drastic severing of relations," if it isolates—and being crucified all the more—something different is at work here. With Jesus, Williams went on, "it is through death that a new and potentially infinite network of relations is opened up. The effect of his death is the opposite of isolation."[25]

And instead of driving him from memory, this death began to endear Jesus even more to a watching humanity. For it was a sign not of forsakenness and erasure but a portrayal of sacrificial love.

The trauma transfigures into a story of how love triumphs over death. Over loss. Over our daily griefs. And yes, that truth holds for our breaks with those we love, like when we come across them unexpectedly at a park, online, a lawyer's office, a town hall, or anywhere.

No wonder the resurrection, when it happened, seemed to be the undoing, the making *un*true of the worst that can happen. For, as *The Book of Common Prayer* reminds us, if we are "wonderfully created," we are "yet more wonderfully restored."[26] It's not only a drama here but also a reclamation project for breakage and lostness. We are given possibilities for how to live, how to grow in grace and goodness. All because of the even more astonishing act in the unfolding drama, to which we turn our attention.

SEVEN

HOW WILL GOD MEET ME WHEN HOPE WANES?

One short sleep past, we wake eternally,
And Death shall be no more: Death, thou shalt die!
—John Donne

I DIDN'T KNOW THAT DEATH COULD HAVE, IN A LITERAL way, a bitter taste. Not till my dad died, and Mom and I wanted to see his body one last time.

I missed by mere hours getting back to California in time to sit with him before he finally succumbed to a heart attack. But now, viewing the body, I hoped for at least a symbolic farewell.

After his body was prepared for burial, attendants ushered us into the refrigerated holding room, my dad on a morgue-issue mattress. I leaned down and kissed his forehead. There was something powerful about that moment, holy, even—honoring this body I had known for decades, whose shoulders I had sat on as a toddler, my hands gripping his thick scalp of hair.

And that's when I discovered a sharp reality: Embalming chemicals left an acrid residue on my lips, an unpleasant tang.

The physical sensation pointed to what is, of course, the deeper loss, what the Bible calls the sting of death. Licking my lips stirred again in me our common longing to know that God moves and works in even the hardest things.

Part of what hurt most was my wanting to tell Dad one last time that I loved him, when I couldn't. I had prayed on the plane ride there, asking God to keep my dad alive till I could sit with him in the hospital. It seemed reasonable to ask. I felt there was some final reconciling to be done, especially in light of the break we experienced earlier in our relationship. And there had been no chance for him to tell me about arrangements he'd made for Mom, who was hopeless with finances.

But when I was greeted at the airport terminal by my mom and a friend of the family, I could instantly read in their faces the news I had dreaded: Dad had died, even as I was winging my way home. Death clipped our relational connecting cord, shutting down, *shouting* down conversation. It seemed so *final.*

But the days ahead were not bleak or empty, either. When I look back, I see more about the Christian promise that Jesus not only died but also was raised from death, holding out promise for our own good and flourishing when *we* know loss. What does it mean not to grieve, as one ancient writer put it, as those "who have no hope"?[1]

DO NOT GO GENTLE

I don't mean this to sound glib. When someone, getting to know me, asks me about my family—my mom and dad and brother—I could say that I lost my parents *twice*: Their rejection, first, when they turned me away and boycotted my wedding, absenting themselves for a time. But by *lost* I mean, as people often do when they use the word, that my folks *died*—my dad when he was just sixty-nine and then a few years later my mom. For we feel a loved one residing *here,* and comfortably, reliably in the world, in *our* world—as it should be. But then they are gone.

Our losses happen in all manners and ways. But especially through dying. Of all the turns in life that cause us pain in our threading through life with others, perhaps this is the most drastic. No wonder that death can shock the system and leave us longing for a story with a better ending.

The poet captured the affront that arises in us, as Dylan Thomas addressed his dying father:

> Do not go gentle into that good night,
> Old age should burn and rave at close of day;
> Rage, rage against the dying of the light.[2]

There's a reason the poem resonates in us, with its defiance. It's rooting for life against loss. Death, as my pastor friend Kevin Miller once preached, "is wrenching. It leaves us bereft. Our greatest fear is that our child or loved one will die."[3] Such loss seems indeed, as the Bible calls it, the last enemy—the ultimate negation of the life God created.

But there is a strand in our culture that takes another tack. It wants to see death as the normal, natural completion of any life, a gentle process, a rejoining of an everlasting circle of life, folding into the endless universal cycle. You don't, the idea goes, live beyond your death in any personal sense. And I guess some find thin comfort in the whole scenario of a cog in the universe that grinds irresistibly, tranquilly on. There's a certain logic, I suppose, in submitting to the inevitable, even if the outcome feels a bit mechanical. But a drop returned to the ocean, as another image suggests, well, gets lost in the vastness and stays faceless. "Any so-called comfort," said Kevin, "will be hollow."

No, death is more of an adversary than that. The death we fear for ourselves, the death we mourn in others—its graphic reality makes us flinch. It can even shake our faith. So maybe you wonder, when death stalks, like never before: *Where is comfort?* How might the vast reality of a triune God get personal here in this supremely lonely moment? When hope must withstand one of its biggest challenges?

THE IMPERMANENT INTERVAL

There's another path between raging defiance and soft surrender. A better story for the end of any human life. And a sign of the way we can live in the meantime, in between birth and death, the impermanent interval. One in which nothing less, *no one less* than the Trinity participates.

This is where Jesus' story comes with a blessed reversal. The crucified one's resurrection from the dead in the Gospels rests at the center of Christian faith for all kinds of reasons: confirmation of divinity, triumph over sin and death, vindication of Jesus' mission, a promise of eternal life for God's beloved. But we see at work the whole assemblage here too: all the persons of the Trinity, not just God the Father and Jesus the Son. We see, in ways that surprise me, the more I look, the Holy Spirit, whom we call in the creed the Lord, the Giver of life. Also now the Giver of *hope,* even when the human race must face down death.

The words of the Ash Wednesday service of many traditions, with charred grit traced on the forehead with a thumb or finger in the sign of the cross, also place our loss in this larger setting: "Remember that you are dust," someone says as the ashes are imposed, "and to dust you shall return." Here's the realism. The bitter taste on the lips. The recognition that the human body by itself becomes food for worms, as folks from Shakespeare to Ernest Becker have pointed out, pointedly.[4] Nothing like a cheery sentiment, right?

But the setting of those words reminds us also of another dimension. If the ashes become a "sign of our mortality and penitence," as the Ash Wednesday service says, they also point us to God's gracious gift. We are "given everlasting life." So, if death entered the world in the garden of Eden, snaking through our common frail nature, making dying universal, God has in mind a reversal of such realities.

This is not to peg the Bible's view as some kind of overdone greeting-card sentimentalism. The Christian faith both sees the disarray caused by death more hopefully and takes it more seriously. It paints the remedy more expansively. Yes, death grieves us, terrifies us, rips from us those we love. Eberhard Arnold suggested the Bible "traces the death of the body back to the fact that sin as separation—as division and isolation—has brought a fatal breach into the living cohesion of creation."[5]

Something cataclysmically good must intervene. For we see not only realism but also hope. The graphic nature of moldering in the ground does not negate the counterintuitive, wildly expectant view that's possible. That is one of the gifts of the grittiness of Good Friday's story of Jesus' arduous death. He knowingly traverses the distance that death and sin create. That scene of death *conquered* gives everything—including heartaches full of loss—a new glimmering. For if a breach has been broached, the ending of mortal life now looks radiantly different.

"Where, O death, is your victory?" asked Paul in the New Testament, rhetorically, convinced that the taunt was warranted.

"Where, O death, is your sting?"

"The sting of death is sin, . . . But thanks be to God! He gives us the victory through our Lord Jesus Christ."[6]

THE UNDOING OF DISOBEDIENCE

Paul and some of the earliest Christian thinkers even argued that Christ, a new Adam, undoes the effects of Adam's disobedience, succeeding where the first Adam faltered and failed. Christ substitutes himself, in a way. There is a recapitulation, as church father Irenaeus called it. He meant a big redo. What happened overcame Adam's disobedience. It becomes in human life a supplanting in its place the goodness of Christ. God in Christ does what we cannot do to repair and restore, inviting us to participate in what he accomplishes. This is not to say it is easy. Just that "God's action in Christ," wrote Fleming Rutledge, "is infinitely greater than all the calamities that followed upon the disobedience of Adam."[7]

The story ends not with despair but with the astonished encounters Christ's first followers had with the vanquishing of death. Jesus appeared in full-orbed presence. No one witnessed the moment of resurrection itself, the instant of the animating again of what had been scourged and pierced and robbed of life. But the times Jesus showed up had such concreteness—with a dose of mystery—that the disciples were jerked out of their deflated fears and buoyed with staggering assurance. The women first, then the apostles, *saw* the risen Jesus. No figment here. This Jesus could appear through walls and locked doors, but he also ate with them, bread and fish. He had them touch the scars from the wounds to confirm the realness. Everything was different. Turned upside down. And yet right side up.

A HAND UP

Easter icons of Eastern Orthodoxy sometimes show the resurrected Christ taking Adam and Eve's hands to pull them up from their graves, drawing them out of the coffined kingdom of death. In one icon version Jesus grasps Adam's hand while Eve's hands are spread wide in open supplication, in waiting and, one can imagine, trembling joy.

I'm going to try to spend time gazing on that scene, taking it in. Or maybe you, in your quiet time reflecting, could let such a prospect push out the littleness of your meditations on who God is. The *what* God can do.

For we see God's love in the empty tomb, not just the cross. We know the Spirit had a hand. And like the crucifixion, it was more than *showing* or exhibiting that love. Easter morning embodied it. Enacted it. God is not only love among the triune persons of the Trinity; we see God as love in the whole drama of birth and death, and now, all the more, death and resurrection. God is love *toward* us. God is love toward us in all that he willingly endured and all that he powerfully made real—the event that transmuted the cross from humiliation to glory. And stands then, for us, as both sign and invitation to a life brimming with, well, *life*.

THE BIG COMEBACK

I've written elsewhere about what Jesus' comeback from the dead means for our looking toward an afterlife.[8] How, for the believer, death opens onto a new world. "Here we do not have an enduring city," wrote a New Testament writer, "but we are looking for the city that is to come."[9] If you have moved around a fair amount, as I have, both as a child and adult, the thought of an enduring eternal city—doesn't that hold great appeal? But even more, we experience the great relief of our faith in that we never again have to live with a fear of eternal rejection. God will not get exhausted by our sin. God will not run out of patience, which isn't to say we don't long for a more holy life.

We have only to look at what God—Father, Son, Holy Spirit—accomplished to see how diligently, daringly God works to heal the destructive effects of sin and death. The goal of the cross and resurrection was not just merciful forgiveness but also reconciliation—not just fixing what's wrong but establishing life, restoring when we think we see creation's slide back to chaos.

If fear of death is our ultimate fear, the resurrection is the ultimate reset: life after being dead, the great release from dread.

God will not get exhausted by our sin.

These foreshadowings of another realm, these rumors of what will come for those who know God's eternal grace, can galvanize something lasting in us. For, wrote the apostle Paul, "we fix our eyes not on what is seen, but on what is unseen, since what is seen is temporary, but what is unseen is eternal."[10] We turn our eyes toward a more glorious view. We recall the scene in the book of Revelation of a "new heaven and a new earth," God residing with his people, wiping "every tear from their eyes," for death will be no more.

MORE THAN WANDERING

God's working in Christ, the Trinitarian participation of the three in Jesus' return to life, means something for my here and now too. Where we are headed affects how we travel. To know that life is not a destinationless journey helps me live more completely for a final good. That the centerpiece of the Christian story is the death and resurrection of Jesus has huge ramifications for daily life. The cross-resurrection is a dual event, a double cure—reversing sin and death's guilt and power. Not only mercy for the past and present but also rekindled hope for how we might live as life unfolds.

Because of intimations of a life beyond, I feel great expectancy and curiosity for what moving through death to a final life will be like. I'm at an age when I know I have far fewer years ahead of me than behind me. But religious faith has always argued that meaning in life is found in part *beyond* life, in a realm where injustice is recompensed, wrong righted, devotion met with deeper joys. The promise of life with God for all time doesn't rob death of its hurt, but it does disarm it of its power to make us cower. The resurrection of Christ is, to use an odd phrase, an advance echo of what we who are known to him can expect.

And whatever its eternal truths, resurrection has an everyday aspect. For it's one thing to feel relief for a past forgiven, healed, and restored. But maybe we still feel bound up and unfree, living under the seemingly irresistible pull of wrong. To some extent, that is the human condition. Or we get trapped in an addiction, perhaps. Maybe you notice some destructive habits in your relating that seem well-nigh impossible to break. Some patterns in how you talk to your spouse or parents or child that you wish you had help for.

Paul, in the epistle to the Romans, gets at this. When we are baptized, he said, there is a sense in which we share in Jesus' death.

We participate in that reality. Troublesome things, the aftereffects of the fall, are plunged under the water. But in baptism we not only die to our old self, we participate in Jesus' resurrection life. We were "buried with [Christ] through baptism into death in order that, just as Christ was raised from the dead through the glory of the Father, we, too, may live a new life."[11]

In a great word some theologians use, we *participate* in the benefits of what Christ has done. We are, as the reformer John Calvin put it somewhere, participants in Christ's own life, in himself. God gives us in him capacity for more than maybe we expected, which means life as we know it opens onto something better than we could have imagined if our own feelings were all we went by.

So we look. We may have to look hard. We may have to rub our eyes and wonder if we are imagining things too good to be true. But that word *look* is key. In a Gospel passage often read on Good Friday, we hear the phrase fall from Pontius Pilate's lips when he presented to the crowd a Jesus who had been whipped, a Jesus crowned with thorns. "Look at the man!" he said. But now that image of the afflicted Jesus transforms. We look again and everything seems different. We wonder about real possibilities, when maybe before we couldn't.

I have a special place in my heart for those who want to believe but struggle—seekers who stand on the fringe and margins, looking on to a community of faith wistfully, thinking they could experience something more, but not sure. I think of a young adult I talked to: "I'm tired of hope," she said. "It just sets me up for disappointment. My life is at a standstill. I feel stuck." Or perhaps faith itself seems flat for some, leeched of any sense of possibilities.

The empty tomb, opening onto a world in which death has been defeated, helps us. Once, preaching on Easter Sunday, I asked, "Wouldn't it be great for Easter to be more than a day but a glorious season in our life together?" For don't we stand—doesn't the world stand—I asked, at the threshold of something new, something to be welcomed? And not just for Sundays?

We practice, some of us, disciplines for Lent—things we do without, the fasting we take on, perhaps good deeds we decide to add. But I sometimes wonder, Why not adopt an Easter discipline? Why not "practice resurrection," as the poet Wendell Berry put it?[12] Why not live with less fear, more joy? And yes, it may take practice.

But God can take even my frailty and mortality and fill it with the permanence of eternity, and plant within me a more durable delight, however many (or few) birthdays I have left. That belief tells me that God will surround my coming and going with life, every day—for all time, and beyond.

THE ETERNITY BEHIND US

Sometimes we think of how the resurrection gives a forward orientation—a future cast to eternity. But there is a background to all this that only strengthens the hope possible: God didn't start being a loving God when humankind came onto the scene. For the Trinity also gives us a backward cast, eternity in reverse, you might say—everlastingly before. Who God is goes as far back as one can go and then some, forever. I mean that the word *forever* not only stretches from now on out but also now *on back.* God has always been, eternally been, as the church teaches, Father, Son, and Holy Spirit. He has for all time been in this triune relationship, in conversation and communal delight. Have you ever thought of all that came *before our own lives* as an amazing backdrop?

Here is where the old idea known as the eternal generation of the Son gains some footing. Jesus' coming derives power and persuasion from the revelation that the three-personed God is directly acting as one throughout the whole story: incarnation, cross, resurrection, and ascension. Our eyes look ahead with renewed hope. But it's also what *was*, not just what will be, that sustains our faith.

"There was never a time," wrote Paul Pastor, "when the Father did not shower the Son with everything he was, never a time when the Son did not give all of himself in return, never a time when the Holy Spirit did not join, blessing and giving and reblessing and regiving, as the very breath of love."[13] The cross did not rupture that. It couldn't. And the resurrection makes the promise shine.

A RESURRECTION WHERE YOU LIVE

Lately I've been struck by what it all might mean for, well, today, even as I write these lines. I think of a couple of sometimes overlooked passages of Scripture, at least rarely truly contemplated by me until recently. But the boldness of what they claim astonishes me, and I've just begun to ponder their import. I can barely take it in. I hope you will begin also to try.

"If the Spirit of [God] who raised Jesus from the dead is living in you," the apostle Paul wrote, "he who raised Christ from the dead will also give life to your mortal bodies."[14] Paul was saying that the power that erupted in the resurrection of Jesus—that cornerstone of Christian faith, that victory over the forces of evil and injustice and death—is moving around, flexing some muscles in the world as we know it. The world as we hope it. It's perhaps simpler to picture it happening in "religious" settings. But Paul is not content to leave the power at work confined to the "spiritual" and "heavenly."

So again, he drove home the point about God's incomparably great power for us who believe. God's power in us and around us, Paul wrote, "is the same as the mighty strength he exerted when he raised Christ from the dead and seated him at his right hand in the heavenly realms."[15] What transpired in the risen Jesus has to do with the everyday, not just the eternal. I forget how *daily* such a truth can feel. God is working in the little things and big. The seemingly microscopic and the massive. Not in some future eternity, but here and now. Everywhere and all the time.

When telling my friend Daniel about my work on this book, the demands, the effort, and the stretching, and in particular this chapter about the resurrected realities of the living Jesus, he reminded me, "That power you are writing about can also move through you and what you write." It got me wondering about how many of our occupations could be infused with a life beyond our own. A vitality that has to do with an eternity that stretches backward and forward and lodges us in a present with possibilities we might otherwise miss or neglect.

I heard about a plumber, active in his church, overflowing with God's life in his own praying, who said as he carried on his trade, "There are some prayerfully laid pipes in this area." I love the picture of a daily life infused with God's risen life.

And I wonder: How might that same power of life look in your daily work and life?

FINDING HOPE IN THE WORST OF LIFE

The picture enlarges too. The violence, the consumerism, the secularism, the cruelty, and the scoffing unbelief that some care so much about: What if we knew that the power of God that raised Jesus from death was also at work in those places? At work renewing us as we try to make a difference? That startling possibility won't happen automatically. The times and places we volunteer, serving the poor, say, or putting time into bringing change to where there is injustice or disregard for those Jesus called "the least of these."[16]

You do the work but then spend time with the Gospel accounts of how God reversed death. You spend time in prayer, letting these resurrection realities seep into your imagination. You have to peer into the shadows of that first Easter morning. How that image of the scourged Jesus gets undone. Death is reversed. Everything is different now. We sense the possibilities.

The New Testament scholar N. T. Wright reflected on how the hopefulness of the risen Jesus helps us:

> What you do in the Lord is not in vain. You are not oiling the wheels of a machine that's about to roll over a cliff. You are not restoring a great painting that's shortly going to be thrown on the fire. You are not planting roses in a garden that's about to be dug up for a building site. You are—strange though it may seem, almost as hard to believe as the resurrection itself—accomplishing something that will become in due course part of God's new world.[17]

We can learn to expect another force at loose. Perhaps not so visible in every fractured family, not in every breakup, not in all the suffering hot spots in the world. But we also think of what Paul called the same strength at work in the resurrection—at work in us. At work in the world. Even just the picture of it can keep us from despair, can refresh something in us.

Once, before our wedding, when I was particularly discouraged by a letter I got from my mom, visiting with Jill that summer we were apart right after getting engaged, I was tearing up. Jill could sense the discouragement I felt.

From some place long ago in her upbringing in a North Dakota Church of the Brethren, Jill reminded me of a song she had learned as a young person: "Turn your eyes upon Jesus, look full in his wonderful face, and the things of earth will grow strangely dim, in the light of his glory and grace."[18] She sang it, a lonely, lovely voice.

I hadn't heard it before, not in my more mainline Methodist church in suburbia. But I listened, and then I joined in.

She wrote the stanza on a slip of paper. For years I carried it around in my wallet, transferring it when one wallet got worn and I got a new one—again and again, until it got too tattered or lost.

I asked Jill recently what made her think of that old hymn. "I knew it's easy to look around and see mainly what devastates us, when we could look up." And as I search for the entire hymn online, I see how it places before us not just the glimpses of Jesus' face. For all its emotional tenor, its potential for too-sentimental piety, it has another vigorous set of lines, something bracing, otherworldly in the best way. There's a setting of sights on what happened back then, when Jesus found himself thrust into the worst darkness and crushing effects of evil in a torturous end. And how with the strength of Trinitarian determination and shared resolve, he moved through:

Through death into life everlasting
He passed, and we follow Him there;
O'er us sin no more hath dominion
For more than conqu'rors we are![19]

The words expressed a hope for me, then—and our ache amid the challenges all of us, at some time or another, will face. They help point me to yet another way in which God draws close, this time especially to help and strengthen. It's time to give the Holy Spirit some attention.

PART 3

OUR GOD HELPS: THE SPIRIT

EIGHT

WHAT IS THIS ELECTRIFYING LOVE?

The descent of the Spirit in the birth of the church is almost like a second incarnation.

—Jason Byassee

Hope does not put us to shame, because God's love has been poured out into our hearts through the Holy Spirit, who has been given to us.

—Paul (Romans 5:5)

I FACETIMED WITH MY BROTHER NOT LONG AGO, A couple of months before Alzheimer's finally took his life. I didn't realize how much more would happen than a typical exchange of news; I also received a poignant reminder. I gained an insight into God's kindness.

We were communicating across a continent—he in California, me in Virginia where I lived at the time. Kevin, recently placed in a nursing home, sat outside in his wheelchair, basking in the sunshine. He couldn't quite navigate the phone, so Angel, his wife, stepped in as a kind of human tripod, holding it up.

As soon as Kevin saw my face, he beamed. Pointing at the screen, he turned to Angel, excitement tinged with confusion and said, "I like that person! He's a nice person."

Angel and I laughed in a good-natured way. Who wouldn't appreciate being recognized as "nice"—even if my brother wasn't dead certain who I was? And he was understanding something deeply important, a long-shared history, dimmed though his command of it seemed. Our screens bridged more than one kind of distance.

"He really loved you, Tim," Angel reflected later, "even if he didn't call you often." Her kind words felt like a gift, especially with all the tough times earlier. But now I was watching him slip away.

Earlier, before his mind grew quite so muddled, I sat with Kevin, gazing out a picture window in his home. He saw the hilly crags in the distance across a valley and imagined patterns or shapes, kept pointing.

"Look—a nickel," he'd say. I'd squint and see a rocky semblance to the face of Thomas Jefferson—yes, *related* to a nickel that bears the former president's face: Like a child or wistful adult tracing shapes in cloud formations, he pointed with delight.

And there was one time when our years of being related were, perhaps, in the back of his mind, though what he said came out garbled: "Her mother died."

"Whose mother?" I asked.

"The student's mother died. They had to check the lines."

Did he mean *our* mother? The IV lines when she was hospitalized? I'll never know. I was watching him mentally slip away.

Because we long so much for communion, wanting to make contact when you cannot becomes one of our hardest experiences. This is what I meant when I mentioned a poignant reminder. We struggle to connect amid all the things that keep us apart—not just physical distance but also other human realities: dementia, estrangement, misunderstandings, perceived slights, sheer forgetfulness. We do our best—or sometimes bring our worst—to understand another and to be understood.

Human relating is notorious, of course, for crossed signals. What challenges we face! Impaired physical speech is sometimes the least of it—especially when there's willful refusal to get along, or when a face turns away. The breakage often happens, of course, with those we love. I confess that when I'm mad at someone I'm close to, sometimes my frustrated anger derails our efforts to talk and listen. Or an outburst causes hurt. Or I may be tempted to write a person off who disagrees with me.

Sometimes you explain and another simply cannot or will not understand. Why will this person not even *try*? When I wanted to defend to my parents the depth and joy of my relationship with Jill, their dismissal was so categorical: They wouldn't hear any of it. They couldn't even entertain the possibility that Jill and I might forge a good life together.

People let us down, by accident or on purpose. They cause us grief. They leave us frustrated. Still, we keep trying to connect. We want to push through the limits of what we try to articulate. We may struggle like Kevin more than we like to think. We want to connect on a deep level, contrary to all the forces that keep us apart and rob our hope.

WHEN DISTANCE DOGS OUR PRAYING

This longing to connect with others better is not only part of life but an inescapable part of faith too. Our relational yearnings inevitably spill into spiritual matters, into our life with God. We have times of exuberance and jumping-up-in-our-places delight, days when the word *ecstatic* seems no exaggeration. God seems so close! But distance sometimes dogs our praying, too, and follows our onetime experience of intimacy with God. So we run into times we need assistance from a power and Presence we can barely see or name. We ask for help even in our wanting God. As in, "God, help me to pray!"

Even when we've had rich moments of praying, most of us must also pass through feelingless, arid stretches with God. It's like we're trapped in the same struggle my brother must have faced, when he sensed his words tangling up on their way out, his mind tripping up, but his heart yearning to reach out. But this time I mean our struggle on a celestial scale. Our words to God choke on our throat's dryness—like a sentence started but forgotten before we can finish. The connection with our heavenly Father feels beyond our reach even before we start. Our intimacy with the living Jesus wanes.

If you have spent much time praying at all, I'm pretty sure you know what I mean. So yes, you try to go beyond mere formality with God, and you experience moments when God is as close as your breath; the intimacy Jesus promised his followers seems yours. "I am my beloved's and my beloved is mine" goes the line from the Song of Songs, a book in the Bible often seen as an allegory for the intimate love God makes possible.[1] But then the feelings grow shy. In those moments, our hearts resemble an arid space where little grows and nothing stirs. I have written elsewhere of how we navigate such dark or dry times with some simple practices.[2]

But some of this frustration may arise from how we picture God, from our anxiety on some days that God has gone into hiding or, worse yet, deserted us. I recall a time when Jill and I were spearheading a new church plant in the suburbs of Houston and it wasn't going as well as we'd hoped. It was barely *going.* God seemed in a mood to ignore our yearning prayers. As I wrote in my journal one day, part of my devotional routine, "I awoke feeling mad at God. I didn't want to pray or read Scripture. I saw my Scripture memory verses by the bedside, and an image of me throwing up flashed through my mind. I thought of praying several times during the day but recoiled at the idea. My anger—or desire to keep God at a distance—paralyzed me."

I share a story like that not to suggest we greet God with churning stomachs but to admit how we can lose the intimacy and intensity. The warmth vanishes. "The disorientation of the lost sense of God," Strahan Coleman wrote, "distraction and hardness in prayer, a bleak self-consciousness of our own sin and brokenness and the disappearance out of nowhere of the experiences of God that enliven us. It's painful. . . . [We have] a sense of God's being 'somewhere else.'"[3]

What we thought promised feasting instead delivers only stale bread. Again, how we picture God can cause us to stumble: God is up there, and here I am just, well, *down here.* Remember the fear that we haven't "measured up"? How it can leave us thinking that God is holding himself at arm's distance? When feeling inept or forgetful around God, maybe we too quickly raise our hands to volunteer to take blame?

All of this makes what I see in the Holy Spirit reviving, a holy breath of fresh air. Here is where "theology" etches onto human hearts a life-giving invitation. What we believe doesn't just satisfy an intellectual itch; it bowls us over. For the Trinity reminds us how God has more relatability up his sleeve than maybe we assumed. We look for what someone called a strength on the inside that somehow seems to come from the outside—not quite a superpower, but supernatural help, assistance beyond our little resources.

Here I am finding encouragement, a sense of going deeper (or getting lifted higher), prodding me to be open, more trusting. Does that possibility sound as attractive to you as it does to me? Wouldn't a given day seem different if we can open our eyes to a splash of delight and hope in the hard and harsh moments? What if underneath it all is a subterranean-rumbling presence that can empower us for what we face? A high-wattage burst of light and life?

We've seen in this book's unfolding story how deep in our bones we yearn for more than a specter or vague force. The Father and the Son give us great help here.

But we may grow wary when it comes to welcoming the Spirit. Maybe we've heard people talk about him in ways that seem mysterious or woo-woo. When we haven't seen the possibilities for something more engaging, we may, as some theologians suggest, settle for a kind of binitarianism. That is, the Father and Son are *persons* in the Trinity, while the Holy Spirit is more like a quality or force. Off to the side. Not part of God's graciously kind ways to make us know we are beloved.

We lose the sense of Scripture and Christian tradition of the Spirit as a lively, life-giving, electrifying *Presence*.[4] Intensely powerful, yes, but intimately personal, too, because here also is the solicitous God we've come to know as one who makes us and holds us. "God's love has been poured out into our hearts through *the Holy Spirit*," Paul wrote in Romans.[5] And not a Spirit floating in some "ethereal sphere" but here, because that Spirit, he said, "has been given to us." You and me. Who says the Spirit does not still move?

LESS THAN FULLY REAL?

But we may struggle with the third Person. As a church member once confessed to me, "With the Father and the Son, we speak of a face. They *seem* like personal beings—I could picture God as a Father, making the world, Jesus as a Son: I could look at his life and miracles and he seemed real, coming bodily to earth. I can relate to that. But the Spirit? That seems more vague."

With the first two Persons, we take in the family-feel language of parent and child; it all carries a kind of warmth and invitation. We picture the Creator tenderly making or speaking gently to Jesus when John the Baptist baptized him: "You are my beloved Son." Or we've heard somebody—or a bumper sticker, unconvincingly—say, "Jesus loves you." I think of Brennan Manning talking of the "relentless tenderness of Jesus."[6]

With the Spirit, our thinking seems to get, well, more airy. Maybe in church we sang "Jesus loves me." But have we lost the gift of expecting life and love from the Spirit?

This is no impersonal or spooky ghost. The Christian tradition gives us a picture of a presence that grieves when we stray,[7] that assures us when we grow anxious, that comes so intensely close we may quake or skip or well up with tears.

The Trinity, I believe, helps us here again: the *whole* picture of Father, Son, and Holy Spirit. I understand my friend's wrestling. Maybe he speaks for you too. But if early in my life, I met God as a kind Father and later Christ the Son as caring rescuer, later still I found myself turning toward the third person of the Trinity. I should say, I suppose, discovering the Spirit turning toward *me*. Showing up. I could feel his presence.

In many ways, it was simple to seek help, to hope for the Spirit to make even more vivid what I'd experienced of God. It didn't, by the way, have to follow in that sequence—Father, Son, and Spirit. The way I've structured this book with a section on each of the Three isn't making a statement about a necessary sequence or order. And I do not mean the heresy of modalism, which, said the early church, confines God to roles, to a kind of limiting job description for each of the three. No, the Three belong together, even if we sometimes scrutinize each for particular activities.

Lest this all seem to veer into the arcane world of academics with elaborate words like *pneumatology* or *coeternal*, or rest only in the reserve of Holy Ghost preacher flamboyance, I've been discerning something simpler, more engaging and inviting, more tied and tethered to everyday living. And not only real but present. The Holy Spirit himself helped the early church figure out how the Spirit played a massive part in their experience of God in Christ—their experience of God's astonishing love in Christ.

When Jesus sat with his disciples for their last supper, he spoke of leaving them: "I am going away. . . . I am going to the Father."[8] He said in effect, "I will leave, but also leave myself with you—in and through the Spirit."[9] While one of the key terms for the Spirit is *breath*, it is the breath of *love*, and that love comes as and comes from a divine Person. In the mysteries of the heavenlies, God reveals not vision-clouding mists but a love shared between Father and Son and Spirit. The Spirit is not a third-position stand-in or gentle by-product of God, but a vibrant Person in his own right.

Wouldn't the Spirit, then, come not with vagueness but with galvanizing epiphanies—an electrifying new vitality? The testimony of many believers is that the Holy Spirit is the most "intimate 'contact point' between the triune God and human beings."[10] Here is a force to reckon with to convince us, against our worst doubts, that we are loved. That we are not alone. That we face anything *accompanied* by a grand Another. And the Spirit helps make that all real, vivid.

I've long been struck by an out-of-the-way couple of verses. They sit in a chapter brimming with other promises that often get the most attention—often read at funerals, for instance, for the promise that nothing shall separate us from the love of God in Christ. We hear the verse about all things working together for good for those who love God.[11]

But I see something else astonishing in what precedes this—verses that depict a spanning power at work, a suggestion that ordinary life is shot through with God's ability to move, act, and transform. I see how much the Holy Spirit breathes through our very words, gasps, and cries—and helps:

> In the same way, the Spirit helps us in our weakness. We do not know what we ought to pray for, but the Spirit himself intercedes for us through wordless groans. And he who searches our hearts knows the mind of the Spirit, because the Spirit intercedes for God's people in accordance with the will of God.[12]

How much gets suggested here! A Spirit who personalizes our prayers with his own wise embellishments? Yes: a Presence who prays through us, in us—*for us.* Bringing in and through his help the presence of God and Christ. With the force of love itself.

THE SPIRIT GOES BACK—WAY BACK

We may think of the Spirit, if we know much about the Bible, as a gift on Pentecost, the early church's going public in power and dynamism as described in Acts 2.

But the Spirit's moving goes back. Way further back. I'm even more impressed by the Spirit when I think of this eternal pedigree. You don't get much more "in the beginning" than the creation of the universe. As far as that goes, we are talking *before* the beginning. When God created the universe, "Earth was a soup of nothingness, a bottomless emptiness, an inky blackness," according to one translation. And here is the crucial addendum: "God's Spirit brooded like a bird above the watery abyss."[13]

This *Person* —not an it—[14] had a hand in bringing order, depth, and beauty where chaos had reigned. We see someone who not only hovers but tends, as the Spirit shows the kind of attentiveness you would expect from a personal Being. Even in the beginning of everything, the Spirit breathed over the waters of what was about to be made. Scholar Sarah Ruden, after her long years of translating ancient texts, said the Spirit broods here, "like a bird over its eggs or hatchlings." God is "above the face" of the water in the sense of "being in the presence of someone or something."[15]

There's more. God breathed—echoing the breath imagery behind the word *Spirit*—breathed *life* into Adam's nostrils, and dust became living matter, mud became flesh. This was not just biology but a joltingly personal act. The Spirit brought life. No wonder the Nicene Creed, which many Christians recite every Sunday, calls the Spirit "the Lord, the giver of life."[16] And why Jesus told his followers, "The Spirit gives life."[17]

Creation brims with a creative dynamism that upholds the first humans' impulses to work and create in their own right. And the Spirit is especially interwoven with that. From before our beginnings, this Person shared with God the impulse to fashion and make beauty. The same breath that breathed life into Adam and Eve kept blowing, kept infusing life. "The breath blows on everything," wrote Clark Pinnock, "bringing life from death, beauty from ugliness, and peace from confusion. The Spirit infuses the world with love."[18]

As the story of God's people unfolds, the Spirit keeps stirring. If the word in the original Hebrew can mean both breath and wind, we then see here a breathed Presence and breeze-driven movement. It often comes with power and seemingly superhuman ability, as when it rested on leaders in early Israel called judges, or prophets in a way that gave extraordinary insight and foresight.

And David the king felt more-than-human eloquence when he declared, "The Spirit of the Lord spoke through me; his word was on my tongue."[19] "Do not cast me from your presence," he prayed elsewhere, "or take your Holy Spirit from me."[20]

And the Spirit fueled God's people's expectancy for the coming Messiah—not so much as a conquering hero but as a suffering savior, moved and motivated by love. Looking forward to the ministry of Jesus Christ, Isaiah the prophet looked ahead and proclaimed,

The Spirit of the LORD will rest on him—
the Spirit of wisdom and of understanding,
the Spirit of counsel and of might,
the Spirit of the knowledge and fear of the LORD—
and he will delight in the fear of the LORD.[21]

Joel even envisioned yet more of the Spirit's vitality:

And afterward,
I will pour out my Spirit on all people.
Your sons and daughters will prophesy,
your old men will dream dreams,
your young men will see visions.
Even on my servants, both men and women,
I will pour out my Spirit in those days.[22]

The early church could not read such passages without thinking about what they witnessed in Jesus—even from the beginning of his story. The Spirit is obvious even in the events relating to the birth of Christ; Mary conceived when she was "found to be with child from the Holy Spirit."[23]

The Spirit appeared at Jesus' temptation. At his baptism the Spirit descended in the form of a dove, nerve-tinglingly present. The Spirit was key in Jesus' resurrection, too, as we've seen: Jesus, though put to death on the cross, was "made alive in the Spirit."[24] Paul burst out with an acclamation that the Holy Spirit was the life at the heart of Jesus' resurrection: "That [Spirit's] power is the same as the mighty strength he exerted when he raised Christ from the dead."[25]

And of course, we look on the scene at Pentecost in Acts 2, when the Spirit released those first preachers from their doldrums and propelled them to burst onto the scene. Open-air preaching electrified the crowd, leading bystanders to assume the speakers had had too much to drink, so intoxicated did they seem with joy—with God's love. Given the decidedly human raw material of their gifts and upbringing and education that is saying something.

Many of the images for the Spirit on that day are concrete and even visceral: fire; a dove descending; a blustery, even violent, wind. The disciples can't sit still or stay quiet. We see the Spirit charge the air with an energizing voltage. The words of the earliest disciples ignited with fire. You would have felt hair-on-your-neck-standing-up sensations. If they came around today, they wouldn't just spread the word; they'd set off smoke alarms.

Maybe best of all, the Bible calls the Spirit the Advocate. Here is where the Spirit means not only that we are helped along but that we are loved through every moment. The Advocate is someone in your corner when things get hard. If we give the Spirit third place, short shrift, Jesus promised the Spirit as a heart-jabbing, heart-filling gift. The effects are sometimes gentle, other times lavish. This supposedly "shy" member of the Trinity can overwhelm our souls with immediacy. The Spirit can move us from where we've been stuck, pierce our bubbles of isolation, and help incorporate us into the communality and the life of the Trinity.

I love how Jürgen Moltmann named the Holy Spirit "Love's Breath."[26] And this dimension, when experienced, can lead to a new sense of competence in place of weariness, a deeper capability to love others in place of wariness. It might look like what some call contemplative or charismatic, more vocal or other times quietly communal.

But whatever the effects left in the Spirit's wake, we find life filled anew with knowledge of our belovedness, making us, in ways we might not yet imagine, filled full.

WHAT TILTS US TOWARD HOPE

In the Gospel of John, as Jesus is talking to his disciples and the air is charged with his insistence that he is about to leave them, about to *die*, and he promises the Advocate, he knows their memories may fog over with some of what he's said, as much as it stood their souls at attention when they heard it. The most vibrant fellowship wrapped up in ministry they've ever known is about to slip through their confused grasp: "All this I have spoken while still with you. But the Advocate, the Holy Spirit, whom the Father will send in my name, will teach you all things and will remind you of everything I have said to you."[27]

And much, when we think about it, tilts us toward hope here. The term Jesus used for the Spirit as he neared his death contains highly personal qualities. There is so much continued intimacy promised, as though the Spirit himself has an open ear, just as Jesus did. A friend of mine told of his practice of receiving Communion every Sunday, then, leaving the altar rail, turning in the quiet of his heart to the Holy Spirit to share his concerns and needs, asking, as he walks back toward his pew, for help. "I can totally see that," I said. I encouraged him to keep at it, to turn directly to the Spirit, for what the Spirit can do and bring. We want a powerful companion. Comforter. Healer. One able to take our God-given gifts and aptitudes and make them flourish and shine.

And so I wonder, how might you open facets of your life to the Spirit, inviting him to make a difference? Can't the Spirit mediate God's love in Christ in our day too? Your day?

And we hear from Scripture how much help we have. We see disciples given astonishing gifts as they continue their preaching missions beyond that Pentecost outbreak. Abilities beyond anything they could muster on their own. I envision an enabling that comes from the Spirit: Whole sections of the New Testament (three in particular[28]) detail so-called spiritual gifts, some that operate with unnerving power and others with unassuming subtleties, all given to help the church help those who are drawn into the family of God. Speaking in tongues or giving meat and bread to a hungry neighbor.

If we need help with a faith that may no longer speak to us, the early church realized that the Holy Spirit came with the vividness and power and potency of God. Might we not follow their example more in asking for such help? Here is not just the vague aura or lingering scent of a person who dropped by, but something definite, left by the presence of someone profound. And absolutely essential for a life immersed in God's love.

We turn to the Spirit ourselves, saying, "Come, Holy Spirit." Or, like Clark Pinnock, "Welcome, Holy Spirit! . . . Breathe on these dead bones, fill us with hope, lead us into God's embrace."[29] When we aren't being so darn careful, we find ourselves wanting to be—pardon the word play—Holy Ghosted.

FULLY HOLY, FULLY GOD

The early church came to realize that it had a number of reasons to believe Jesus and his Father were, as Jesus said, one. But once the councils clarified how Jesus was fully God, fully human, and God incarnate, the *Spirit* needed attention and articulation. Some in the day of Athanasius said the Holy Spirit was merely an angel. Divine, yes, somehow, but not truly God. From, in other words, another realm—a heavenly place—but created by God and therefore inescapably inferior. A celestial add-on, but not exactly built into the core of God's life of relatedness.

Athanasius wouldn't have it. Just as the Son was and is and will be eternal, so also, he argued, "the Spirit is not a creature since he exists eternally with the Word and is in him." He is worthy to be "glorified along with" the Father and Son.[30] Worthy of worship. And not content with that, Gregory of Nazianzus made an unequivocal declaration that the Holy Spirit, as part of the Trinity, is *God*. The bishop offered himself to the almighty Father, the only begotten Word, and "the Holy Spirit, who is God."[31]

For the Spirit, the disciples and earliest followers of Jesus discovered, came to them not as a bumbling emissary from a distant land but as the real article. Yes, some distinction, but not separate from God—rather, God. He did what God did. And not just in thimblefuls, but as inexpressible, infinite power. The nearness and power of God himself, leaving trails of ecstasy and healed lives and people aroused and awake to the love of God in Christ. And the Spirit-inspired singing that could break down prison doors gave an eloquence to otherwise unsophisticated street preachers. Supplied words to the early followers jotting down the stories of Jesus. Had people crisscrossing the known first-century world to be used by God to do surprising things. Used by God to change the course of history.

A MORE VISCERAL FAITH

Sometimes, to live profoundly, to let the Spirit move through you more, you do something extraordinary. Perhaps you have, in your longing pilgrimage through life. Emily Dickinson did so, closeting herself away in pursuit of her creative passion. Emily—mysterious, brilliant, afire with devotion—wrote poetry that pulses with discoveries of a more vivid, visceral faith. "Your thoughts don't have words every day," she admitted:

> They come a single time
> Like signal esoteric sips
> Of the communion Wine[32]

She stumbled, wasn't sure of her gifts some seasons, wasn't sure about *God* some days, but also sensed a creative intensity surging through her and her writing. She more than once described herself as a smoldering volcano, so passionately did she experience her calling. And she turned again and again to God, for all her shyness toward regular churchgoing and institutional church matters. She knew: Artists and writers and musicians often sense the ecstatic and electric overtake them, in ways sometimes similar to the saints' exhilarating spiritual experiences.

"When I painted as a child," the artist and author Makoto Fujimura wrote, "I felt as if an electrical charge were going through me. That energy resounded over the surface of the paper. I thought everyone had this experience." When Makoto later became a Christian, with new eyes and a transformed heart, he concluded, when "I created and felt that charge, I was experiencing the Holy Spirit."[33]

And Emily would say Amen. "My little Force explodes," she wrote to her future editor and erstwhile mentor Thomas Wentworth Higginson.[34] This was 1862, when she was firing off some three hundred poems a year, some of them jotted on scraps of discarded envelopes, unfolded and spread out.

Her passionate commitment was different from that of Julian of Norwich. They both shared a reclusive tendency. A passion to pray and write and tend to special gifts, yes, but Emily was far from as church-centric, for one thing, as her medieval predecessor. Still,

Dickinson's poetry grew out of a sometimes wistful estrangement and a frequently passionate engagement with God. She might wonder about and even poke God with her questions, but she couldn't shake or push down her yearning for God. Or the sense that a spiritual force was visiting her when she wrote. It was different from what you see in the followers of Jesus on the day of Pentecost, but still full of a power that has spoken across the generations.

Once while in New England, I visited Emily Dickinson's house, now restored and preserved as the Emily Dickinson Museum. I saw, while visiting her historic home, a facsimile of Emily Dickinson's writing desk, set by windows in the corner of her bedroom, seventeen by seventeen inches square, the size of a mere chessboard. She sometimes wrote with a stubby pencil on any scrap she could find. But that single-hearted passion, both for her art and God! She lived deeply, not only to write verse but to sit with God.

And she moved through her daily household duties immersed, at least some days, in a world enchanted by the overarching Presence, delighting in her glimpses of God, an encounter made vivid, according to Christian belief, by the Holy Spirit. She wistfully imagined a God knocking on her sometimes pushed-shut door, and she pleaded, "'Oh, Jesus . . . / I'm knocking everywhere.'"

"From our vantage point more than a century later," wrote Roger Lundin, Dickinson "stands as one of the major religious thinkers of her age."[35] Quirky Emily, the Belle of Amherst, largely reclusive, who pleaded, for all her wonderings, "Infinitude, hast thou no face?"[36] Who lived not just with a holy bafflement but also a determination to stay in the game even when God seemed distant.

I think with hopefulness about Emily's calling, tentative though she might sometimes have been. The Spirit can invest our efforts to serve, create, speak, write, lay pipes, and worship. There was more than soberness and seriousness in her. Also joy, when the comforts of the Holy Spirit's presence showed up in the play of words, the ways words could become vehicles for expressing what cannot be expressed. When she sensed God inhabiting her words and the home of her heart.

HOW THE WORDS COME

Several years ago, a young friend joined me in what soon became a mutual quest. A high school senior, Ben was wondering about Christianity, which he had briefly rebelled against. He showed up at the church where I pastored one Sunday and explained his questions. I, too, felt drawn to a more profound experience of faith and serving. A greater depth in praying too. I look back now and see how much his quest reflected what many of us long for. Does his longing remind you of your own?

Not long after he began coming, Ben attended a large regional youth conference. One of the workshop leaders encouraged attendees to meet with a pastor or church leader regularly for Bible study when they returned home. Ben got back and asked if we could get together once a week.

As we met, I found that Ben had the springtime faith of a convert. His enthusiasm needed grounding and maturing, but his eagerness was contagious—especially when it came to prayer. Unbothered by the finer points of theology, he simply wanted to experience as much of God's presence and power as he could. I found my own longing for a deeper experience of prayer challenged and encouraged by Ben's energy. We spoke not only of Christ's mercy but also of the ways the Holy Spirit might help us.

My young friend, whom *I* was supposed to help, became a catalyst for my own growth.

One February afternoon, with a longing for a new spontaneity and fluency in prayer and a desire for a breakthrough in my prayer life, I got into my car after visiting someone from my church who was hospitalized, and I started praying about my praying.

From within, it seemed, streamed an intensity of praise to God and a communion with him not bound by words. Have you ever experienced an electric fervor without really trying? I sensed a flowing, powerful joy. Syllables formed new combinations beyond my conscious formulations or comprehension, and they were carried along, it seemed, by a force welling up. Some people would call this "speaking in tongues." Some, less inclined to root events in the working of the Spirit, would say I gave voice to a primal speech arising from subterranean depths. Others might point to contemplative graces that come to those who sit waiting in God's presence.

I know that careful words seemed inadequate for the depth of what was happening within me. When Paul the apostle contrasted "praying with my mind" and "praying in the Spirit" in the New Testament, I think that is at least partly what he had in mind.[37] The Spirit can lift our praying beyond words, carrying our hearts to a communion and wonder that language cannot capture. The experience brought a depth and fluency in praying that has rarely been far from me ever since.

I wonder if all this talk of the Spirit might help you discover a deepening awareness of the divine side of prayer. I mean by that that you will care less about articulating everything just so and instead open yourself more and more to the One who first comes close to us in grace. One who continues to help us by his presence, by his willingness to shape our words. When it comes to prayer, our spiritual impulses don't always need words—especially when carried along and spoken through us.

And the Spirit points us to Jesus, just as Jesus spoke with anticipation of the Spirit's coming once he left the disciples. Elizabeth Oldfield told of becoming a Christian through an "ecstatic encounter" in her teens. "At a youth festival I had been invited to by a churchgoing friend, I prayed, 'God, if you are there, would you show me?' and then spent an hour (or five minutes?) flat out on the floor of the arena. I can't tell you what happened in that time, because it was beyond language, but I stood up a Christian, changed at what felt like a cellular level."[38]

We cannot force such moments. But we can wait. We can prepare the ground by staying open, caring about living a holy life, and submitting ourselves in obedience. And then from time to time, quite often when we least expect it, God will give our prayers flight. What had been a discipline becomes a delight. Our stumbling words are lifted into song. We "pray in the Spirit,"[39] to use Paul the apostle's phrase, lofted above the normal constraints. The love of God, our belovedness, takes a new dimension. We feel a new capability to respond. Yes, there will be dry spans, very likely, at some point. It won't always feel like an electrifying time at the desk or kneeling in church.

But while we often talk about the love of God in Christ, we may forget how willingly the Spirit comes by. The Spirit tenderly helps us. Coaxes us. Makes possible the times when prayer "takes off." Thomas Kelly, for example, was a quiet Quaker scholar who decades ago penned a spiritual classic called *A Testament of Devotion*: "There come times when prayer pours forth in volumes and originality such as we cannot create. It rolls through us like a mighty tide. Our prayers are mingled with a vaster Word, a Word that at one time was made flesh. We pray, and yet it is not we who pray, but a Greater who prays in us."[40] A Greater who prays in us and who places us in God's presence, immersed in a greater Love.

That is the testimony of others through the centuries—poets and priests, preachers and teachers, scholars and students—some you'd think would be the *most* articulate, knowing that God's Spirit stands ready to pray through them, giving mere words flight. Giving voice to gratitude for how God gives us more than we ask or imagine.

MORE THAN SWEAT AND CLEVERNESS

One of the Christian tradition's favorite words for what the Spirit is, does, and brings is a simple one: gift. The *gift* of the Holy Spirit. The *gifts* of the Holy Spirit. The ways his power in us leave us *gifted* for what we could not achieve on our own. The way our belovedness in Christ becomes something we are enabled to share.

Out for a run one morning, I thought about needing to pick up the writing pace for this book. It seemed to be going well—at least the hours at a desk weren't making me want to throw my laptop out a window. But I felt that normal, nagging sense of not-enoughness we often feel in big endeavors. More than high-octane caffeine and pep talks were in order. I could feel the weight of the manuscript deadline, too, a date already extended once. This was not, I knew, something to achieve simply with mere sweat and cleverness.

With one part urgency and another part expectancy, I felt moved to pray. I felt moved to turn to the third Person: "Come, Holy Spirit!" It's a solidly biblical prayer and in those moments it felt like a supremely useful ask.

Instantly I felt a lightness. I seemed lifted along as I jogged. Such a simple prayer, and critical: "Come!"

I got back to the house and found a text from my friend Kevin Miller: "Tim, I am praying for you this morning that you will be given the wind of the Spirit at your back as you write."

Which leads me to repeat yet another favorite term for the Spirit in Scripture: helper. Not mechanical assistance, not artificial ticking off of ordered steps, but something far more personalized: something related to the lives we live and the challenges we face. At our backs or coming from above, what could encourage us more than God showing up to help? Right where we live? Making us able?

And lest I give the impression that it's all about individual devotion and solitary prayer, there's more to say about the Holy Spirit's electrifying presence. More about the love the Spirit gives us in showers of blessing. I mean something that helps us help others. The Helper becomes our hope to make a difference in a hurting world. I mean fortifying assistance that comes to a group and turns it into a movement. I mean a personal impact that visits a gathering and makes it a force for change. That takes a table we gather around and transforms what happens there into a world of meaning for others who stand far off and who, like us, stand in need of loving help.

NINE

WHAT LIFE IS POSSIBLE WHEN LOVE BLOSSOMS?

The church is the family of God, called to live the baptized life in a world that is rebellious against God and continues to do battle against God's purposes.

—Robert E. Webber

The very purpose of [Jesus'] self-giving on the cross was not just to save isolated individuals, and so perpetuate their loneliness, but to create a new community whose members would belong to him, love one another, and eagerly serve the world.

—John Stott

IT WAS *SO* SOUTHERN CALIFORNIA, BRANDT'S INVITAtion, and it left me with mixed feelings. He looked long-haired and bearded, a Jesus stand-in if there was one, except for the blondish hair and denim. An itinerant minister, he hung around my Santa Monica high school leading Bible studies on the main lawn, cheering on the searching. At his invitation, he and I met weekly at a Denny's to talk. We'd dive into Scripture, unpack the weight of every passage, and I'd leave feeling like I understood more than I expected—and I could tell him anything. Nothing felt off-limits. I know it doesn't always happen, but I hope at some point you've had a friend or mentor play a similar role, someone with whom you can talk about spiritual matters.

"We're doing an ocean baptism," he said one time when we met. It would happen right on the Santa Monica beach not a mile from my house—sands along which I'd often run. He and some of his friends would be right there with the surfers and beach bums, extending kingdom territory. "Why don't you come along? I'd love to baptize you."

I felt drawn to say yes. But when I mentioned Brandt's invitation, my parents sniffed, "You've been baptized!" I couldn't recall it, of course; I was just months old when they took me to the downtown Methodist church in Phoenix that towered above Central Avenue.

And while I'm not sure the leaders at the California church we attended knew what to do with my un-mainline fervent piety, I did attend the church youth group, which seemed more respectable in my folks' eyes.

Still, social ideals and spiritual experimentation were in the air. Brandt and this movement of the early seventies were, as Anne Lamott might put it, more Jesus-y. More exhilarating.

I don't recall a happier time. Mornings I'd awaken with a start, with a pulse of joy. It's hard to describe the sheer delight of discovering Jesus as a daily friend and companion. At Bible studies on campus, breezes blowing off the ocean waters blocks away, we'd read about the Holy Spirit's stirrings in the book of Acts and feel like we could identify. Back then, when the church was young, the Spirit *did* remarkable things, didn't just speak them, sparked wonder and awe, and moved people in the crowds to tears—or fury. The gatherings of Jesus' followers seemed charged with intensity and high-wattage anticipation.

Things would have been more sedate in the suburban Phoenix church where my parents took me as a baby for baptism. Not long ago I called the church to find out more, and the assistant patiently checked their records. The Reverend Bass, a Methodist minister, officiated.

He sprinkled handfuls of water over my tiny forehead, saying, "Timothy, I baptize you in the name of the Father, and of the Son, and of the Holy Spirit." Impressive words for those old enough to understand. Perhaps I at least absorbed the air of reverence in the church's soaring spaces.

We would move away from that city, losing any connection to that congregation, but I've begun to see how that simple baptismal formula, said before several hundred onlookers, some smiling, some dozing, set my family—and my life—into bigger truths of which the baptismal words mostly just hinted.

It also, now, strikes me how profoundly forward-looking that Sunday morning baptism was—long lost to memory as it must be for any infant. Baptism, if you have experienced it, for yourself or another, makes you think of the possibilities for a life splashed with the freshness of water.

If in the mid-fifties American families returned in droves to church, for my mother, who insisted we all attend church and Sunday school, that sacramental ritual was more than form or formality. Something in her fiercely loved spiritual things, clung to them even.

I see that in myself now, at my better moments, a kind of intensity about things mysterious and miraculous that must have somehow seeped into me. Some seeds got planted, helped to germinate by the waters of baptism.

And I know now, as I counsel parents and godparents before a baptism, how it represents a radical act—to place a well-loved child in God's hands and plans, God who is infinite and close by and filled with big plans. It underscores how we are beloved, to be sure. How Christ reaches into our life to save and rescue and make us able to serve. We are "sealed by the Holy Spirit," as many of the baptismal liturgies say, "and marked as Christ's own forever."

But have you ever thought of baptism as a little scary? It reminds us how the baptized are placed in larger hands, graced, as gets said time and again, "in the name of the Father, and of the Son, and of the Holy Spirit." Did my parents realize then that with God working in my life I would be subject to a larger plan? That I could move away, circling back to home and its comforts but also meeting other souls along the way, coming back each time a bit changed?

Nothing would keep me from those Bible study meetings, but in the end I opted out of Brandt's invitation. Some aspects of the traditional church seemed to have a place. Both settings, different as they were, tell me important things about how I've done church, how I inhabit reverent spaces, how I need to be part of something communal and Spirit-lit. I hope you consider your own participation in gatherings of ardent devotion—communities of faith and service. I've never been much drawn to spirituality as a do-it-yourself project. That feels too lacking in a personal touch and real support. I'd rather be among friends, in all the different forms that linking can take. I want to know the life of the beloved among others living out what it means for them, too, to be so deeply cherished.

AN UNCOMMON COMMON LIFE

Words like *fellowship*, *communion*, or *community* come to mind. The New Testament certainly gives an array of glimpses of common life among God's own. We see how receiving—and giving—spiritual friendship stands as essential to growth. Jesus, of course, from the outset of his work surrounded himself with followers, corralling his special protégés and friends—"the twelve"—a small group, not a teaching amphitheater. In the intimate setting of meals, he laid before them his deepest truths, where he stressed how loved by God they were. It was amid the concrete elements of bread and wine that he urged them to love one another.

Amid the piercing drama of his last week on earth, at his last supper with his disciples, he gave them a "new command": to love one another, and to remember him best by sharing around a table, which we sometimes now call an altar.[1] He even stooped, astonishingly, to wash their feet, on the eve of his sorrowing journey to the cross. When the risen Jesus appeared to them, which scared the living daylights out of them, he breathed on them the breath of the Spirit to get them through the next few days. To fill them with the breath and wind of divine love.

But there was more.

The Holy Spirit, for all his fabulous, furious work in the first days after Jesus' resurrection and ascension, did more than buoy them up. He did more than ready them for preaching and teaching, more than helping them recall what he did and taught. He became the giver of life for their life together.

The Spirit moved powerfully where believers lived and shared. The Spirit in their midst seemed not only to pull people together but also to explode them outward. So the tongues of fire and rushing wind of Pentecost, yes, but then this: "[Those hearing the preaching] devoted themselves to the apostles' teaching and to fellowship, to the breaking of bread and to prayer." That sounds intense and pretty communitarian. And yes, "everyone was filled with awe at the many wonders and signs performed by the apostles."

But in the next beat we read: "All the believers were together and had everything in common. They sold property and possessions to give to anyone who had need. Every day they continued to meet together in the temple courts. They broke bread in their homes and ate together with glad and sincere hearts."[2] There was power in the preaching but also a theology in the everyday, as daily needs found fulfillment when people shared their possessions. Love was in the air. There's a hovering sense that the Spirit moved with special power when they *met*. And the Spirit fueled their love for one another—and their love for the world they were about to turn upside down with their service and proclamation.

The epistles written by the likes of Peter and Paul overflow with affection and with assurances that even when the fledgling churches got ensnared in conflicts, still the Spirit moved, addressed their need for help, and brought new life—bringing the kingdom to bear in tangible ways.

THE CIRCLE WIDENS AT PENTECOST

Of course, the Spirit of God is mentioned in the Old Testament; it seems mostly limited to Israel or the temple or special persons called to special purposes.

But at Pentecost the circle widened as the vibrant and expulsive life of the early church picked up common people and swept them into dramatic confrontations with spiritual complacency and evil—and illness, as healings happened. The power that raised Jesus from the dead and appeared in the ascension of Jesus became power for God's people. The love the disciples painfully witnessed and poignantly felt in the crucifixion now propelled them to speak. Pentecost was the day that the once-shell-shocked and sheltered followers found their voice as God's beloved to proclaim the story of God the Father's coming in Jesus and in the power of the Spirit.

The third person of the Trinity comes now not with gentle breath but like the wind that swept across the dark, chaotic waters of unformed creation, as it says in Genesis, bringing life and vitality, this time with everyday followers. "Everything is by wind and fire, loud talk, buzzing confusion, and public debate," said author and pastor William Willimon. Maybe it's a little messy. But the Spirit, wrote Willimon, "is the power which enables the church to 'go public' with its good news, [and] to attract a crowd . . . A new wind is set loose upon the earth, provoking a storm of wrath and confusion for some, a fresh breath of hope and empowerment for others."[3] They soon turned the known world upside down.

But we forget the prelude the Gospel accounts and the book of Acts give us. We see the disciples befuddled, fearful. It's a sorry little picture, actually. John told us, before Jesus' resurrection appearances, the doors of the house where the disciples were meeting had been locked because they feared the religious leaders. Locked from the inside—from the fears that made the deflated followers shake and huddle.

But the disciples were doing something right—meeting *together*, not cowering in lonely corners. And they were praying. And waiting together. They *stayed* gathered. That's the setting. That's when at Pentecost the Spirit was poured out on all believers—young and old, sons and daughters, with open-air preaching missions and smaller gatherings where widows and the needy got cared for. Where bread got shared. Where love spread among them in ever-new ways.

This Holy Ghost scenario can sound challenging to our privately "spiritual but not religious" culture. Solitude off in the woods or hanging out with buddies at the golf links has a place. But here we see how

God will go to great lengths, even a cross, to meet us with kindness and set us in a community of those likewise learning they are beloved.

I'm still not sure we know why we feel so compelled to opt out of friendshipping, to be so removed. I don't see the appeal of walling ourselves up in aloneness, in our increasing antisocial withdrawal. I'm not sure why my parents isolated themselves so much from family when they moved to the West Coast—my dad from Irish working-class Boston, my mom from a little railroad town in Tennessee. It was rare to get a visit from relatives, or for us to visit them. At least we made church a habit.

I see that kind of lonely withdrawal now even more, reaching worrisome loneliness of pandemic levels. We have a habit of overestimating the resources of our own singular selves. "I'd rather do it myself" is more than an advertising jingle from when I was young. We may have a resistance, or at least reluctance, to admit how much we need the help, presence, and love of the Spirit catalyzed among others. We sense a stigma attached to our longing, a tinge of shame if we haven't found the resilience we think we should in our own little selves. We prefer to proclaim, "I am a rock," the title of a popular song from my youth, islanded in our absurd pride.

But I won't find what I most need to grow in my experience of the Spirit if I just "do me" while "you do you," each of us isolated into our perpetual silos. I need constant reminding of how much God cares. And I am prone to forget off by myself. The spiritual life, Robert Webber wrote, "is nourished by the church, which is the continued presence of the incarnate Jesus in and to the world."[4] It is the fellowship of the Spirit. We are created to live in community, not competitiveness. In a society of love, not lonely autonomy. Our souls are made to

We are created to live in community, not competitiveness. In a society of love, not lonely autonomy. Our souls are made to thrive in the company of others.

thrive in the company of others, enjoying the eruptions of the Spirit in our midst:

Two are better than one . . .
But pity anyone who falls
and has no one to help them up.
Also, if two lie down together, they will keep warm.
But how can one keep warm alone?
Though one may be overpowered,
two can defend themselves.
A cord of three strands is not quickly broken.[5]

THE UGLY SIDE OF COMMUNITY

We all know community anywhere can get profoundly messed up, ugly, strewn with emotional body parts. We may not *like* the person next to us in the pew. We may detest the views of someone we take Communion with. Some people serving on church leadership boards say, when learning about the goings-on among staff or the pettiness of some members, they've seen "how the sausage gets made." But what we miss when we stay away!

If the Trinity, with its communal ease and richness, reminds us of a better way, the Spirit makes it possible. He helps us and guides us. When we take walks in our neighborhood I sometimes tell my wife how I've been moved by the picture of God as a warmly interpersonal Being. Not necessarily what you think of as typical domestic chitchat.

"You've always had higher intimacy needs than me," Jill once said when I was talking about my friends, my fascination with a highly relational God, and we laughed at that, recognizing how I bring a need for connection to everything, even to my praying. Even to my getting through life. I fight what I saw in my folks, the isolating tendency, and I know the dismal aftereffects. And I know I need God's love like I need the constant nourishment of food. Like I need the bread of Communion shared in a body of believers.

And it's not just about *feeling* alone; it is also about things that won't get done if we insist on going it alone. It strikes me that Pentecost's—literally—fiery preaching did not happen to individuals off praying all by themselves, but to disciples praying together, waiting as a little knot of hope for the power to come, for the conviction to get so settled in them that they would finally burst out with good news, when finally the Spirit came with tongues of fire.

"AND THERE WAS YOUR NOTE"

Why would we think we don't need support? A man, I was told, was struggling for truth against deceit and prejudice in his city. I don't know all the details. But a colleague in a distant city heard of the battle he was waging and sent him a note of encouragement and concern. He told him he cared and was praying for him. He reminded him that he was beloved, no matter what detractors said.

Some years later, when the letter writer had forgotten about the note he sent, a knock came at his door. There stood the man to whom he had written. "I came to thank you," he said. "I had gotten to the place where I thought I was about to have a breakdown, and my wife and I had agreed I should give up the struggle. We were sitting, demoralized, in our living room when I heard the mail being delivered. I went to the mailbox, and there was your note. God wiped the windshield clean, and I started over again."

I cannot bear my spiritual longings all by my lonesome. I'm not meant to. It is not good for Adam to be alone, God said. It's not good for Christians to stand apart, to shrink back from help from others. I need someone to join a voice with my faltering praying. Someone to remind me to go out in the courage that comes from knowing palpably God's love and to do something risky.

This communal spiritual strengthening takes lots of forms. It usually needs leaders. "We desperately need men and women at our side," wrote Eugene Peterson, "who have disciplined their minds to think *God*: who God is and what he is doing in and among us; what it means to be created and chosen by God and how we get in on what he intends for us."[6]

And we may need to let ourselves be challenged, to have our need for an hour or so of peace on Sunday morning jostled a little by preaching that takes a prophetic turn. If left to myself, my prayers become imbalanced or stuck. If left to myself, my life and my aspirations become like an ingrown toenail. I need a way to avoid letting the eccentricities of my personal faith fester or get me caught in a rut. My moods are too fickle to be reliable guides for the entirety of my spiritual life.

I need the expanding of vision that praying with others brings. That worshiping with others opens up. Prayer needs the soil of community to put down roots. Then we bear fruit, which, like the word *gift*, is another word for what the third person of the Trinity produces in the beloved, the qualities that make life rich: *the fruit of the Spirit*.[7] God tends this harvest as part of his work in restoring a fallen creation.

When I come to worship in a blue funk, it does me good to join in a congregation's choruses of alleluias. I find reinforcement of the good news of God's love. Or I may be feeling pretty complacent about myself and my life, convinced that all is well with the world and me. I need the reminder of prayers of confession that I still stumble and desperately need God's forgiveness—that I have in no way earned my belovedness—not when it is a gift through and through. Perhaps I am too at peace with the world, living as I do in a comfortable house and a pleasant neighborhood. I need, then, to be called to intercession for the world's hungry and poor, those for whom the God of love in Father, Son, and Holy Spirit ever aches. The Spirit will speak through others, wise leaders and common fellow pilgrims.

The Spirit will speak through others, wise leaders and common fellow pilgrims.

And when I feel spiritually dry, I can be carried along by the stream of a corporate reverence. There is help in "being led" in prayer. Someone leading the service not only invites us to pray; the corporate pray-er helps us actually find the words, words that we might never find within our small selves.

Liturgy, the technical word for the way churches order their worship, is *given*—we don't have to devise it continuously, making it up as we go along. We turn to the words and phrases and images of Scripture and tradition—others who have gone before, whose prayers and responses to God bear up well through the test of time, or others who make radiant in real time the truths of faith and prayer.

We know from firsthand experience that churches are complex organisms. And they require, on some days, at least, patience and care and prayer. Even sometimes intervention—mediators or consultants or overseers who can help a congregation move through conflict. We don't overspiritualize the ways any group can become toxic or abusive. But the basic unit of God's moving is mostly a gathered fellowship, a community of celebrating God's love, becoming contagious with praise for God and love for others. A fellowship of the loved and redeemed.

WHEN HEARTS POUR FORTH

Sometimes, in our institutional realities, we forget the moving of the Spirit. I have been a part of a wide variety of churches, traditions, and denominations. But the Spirit longs to work in all of them, sweeping us up where we are, where we pray. I hope you have found such evidence when you consider your places of communion with others.

Sometimes the Spirit moves gently, behind the scenes. Other times he moves more visibly, obviously, like in this analogy: "I play in a symphony orchestra," one internet friend of mine, a person who wants to grow in prayer and her participation in worship, wrote. "There are times when the entire group of eighty musicians becomes inspired—we don't know why—and we play absolutely magnificently. We all say, 'What happened?' No one can answer. It happens in the spiritual life also."

It happens in my praying sometimes. In my worship some Sundays. My heart pours forth its longings without faltering. Sometimes I feel an overflowing love for God or for his goodness or the world God made that leaves behind a scripted word. My normal speech seems limited, so I pray in turned-out longing, sometimes palms upturned becoming in themselves a form of prayer. Sometimes that happens when singing with others, caught up into something swirling around me and within me, something bigger and more uncontained than just little me.

I can only call those moments gifts, foretastes of the communion we will enjoy in heaven.

Duke professor Jeremy Begbie, in his book *Abundantly More*, used a phrase I love: "An Unbounded Rush of Gladness,"[8] and in doing so he told of the fascinating comments Augustine made on Psalm 33:3, the exhortation "Sing to [the Lord] a new song; play skillfully and shout for joy." What are "shouts"? Augustine asked.[9] Does this represent simple, unrestrained exuberance in the presence of God in worship?

It must mean more, the ancient bishop wrote: "It is to realize that words cannot communicate this song of the heart. Just so singers in the harvest, or the vineyard, or at some other arduous toil express their rapture to begin with in songs set to words." Here we are on the terrain of normal hymns or worship songs. But Augustine went on: The workers sometimes find what they sing lifted above and beyond lyrics. "Then as if burst with a joy so full that they cannot give vent to it in set syllables, they drop actual words and break into the melody of jubilation. . . . In this way the heart rejoices without words and the boundless expanse of rapture is not circumscribed by syllables."[10]

This is what Begbie called "praise that overspills the capacities of speech." Such a strange and moving experience "seems especially apt as a mode of praise for a God who, although within the reach of language" will not—cannot—be limited by it.[11]

Old hymns can do it. Contemporary worship songs might. Folky versions of Scripture set to music sometimes capture our imaginations, putting our words in sync with a larger rhythm. They put us in step with the worshiping of others. And I've seen worship services where, unrehearsed and unplanned, a kind of free-form singing begins to move like a wave over the congregation. The musicians leading the music quiet down a bit, and "singing in the Spirit," as the phenomenon is called, can unfold.

There's a simplicity to it and yet also a depth that seems unrestrained by phrases, a release from self-conscious thought, as though mere words no longer tie down to earth what the Holy Spirit stirs and lifts from the heart. And in more liturgical settings it might happen when a kind of holy hush settles over the proceedings. A blessed silence. Or the reverent receiving of the bread and wine of Holy Communion takes on a quality of hushed holiness.

It may look pretty ordinary. There may be moments of tedium in our sitting. But God shows up in the mundane gatherings, helping to fan into flame a hidden hope that life also holds room for the miraculous. We stay on the lookout for reminders of our belovedness.

Maybe the preached Word refreshes our memory of the ways God can intervene and change a dark, difficult situation. Of course, the reality is that we cannot claim for ourselves a sure and certain outcome when we turn and ask and plead. We don't treat intercessory prayers like incantations. But a community fuels expectancy, just enough to keep me hoping but not so much that I can come to think of a dramatic answer to prayer as something I'm owed. Might such liveliness freshly speak to a watching world emptied of enchantment and grandeur? What might the Spirit be waiting in the wings to accomplish when there's renewed openness?

WISTFULLY ASKING

I still ask, "In what sense is God active? How does the Spirit move?" And I wonder, have you found a church community that brings life and renewal? That helps you sense God's love and the caring of God's people? If not, pray for help.

Jill and I came across a book that would spur one such movement. We were longing for something more. On someone's recommendation, we read the published journal of the late poet Luci Shaw, *God in the Dark*. The memoir recounted the illness and death of Shaw's husband. More significantly for us, Shaw chronicled her recent discovery of a church not far from where we lived in a suburb west of Chicago. She wrote often of St. Mark's Episcopal in Geneva, Illinois, where her poetic sensitivities found a home.

I had just joined the editorial staff of *Christianity Today* magazine. We attended an independent church in Wheaton, Illinois, where a colleague had invited us. While we respected the faith and dedication there, we soon grew restless with Sunday morning worship, characterized by little Scripture, a short pastoral prayer, three hymns, and a forty-minute sermon. We encountered a pragmatism that seemed to leave little room for mystery and awe. It hid God's transcendent, glorious *other*ness behind a dry, cerebral approach.

We decided to visit Shaw's church. And from the beginning what we witnessed struck a chord. Here was the outflow of a long stream of worship, witness, and service—a tradition that would not ignore centuries of witness and faith after the canon's formation. I had been discovering the writings of the great classical spiritual life figures: Augustine, Thomas à Kempis, Francis and Clare of Assisi, Julian of Norwich. I also read Thomas Merton's *The Seven Storey Mountain*, about being found by God's love in Christ, and it moved me profoundly. All this opened me to a world that did not cease with the first century, only to resume with the Reformation and leap again to the current century. Now, Sunday after Sunday, I could join in liturgies and spoken rhythms that had ordered the lives of the faithful for generations.

What we found there, and in other churches in a similar tradition, was theologically solid, liturgically Anglican, and influenced by streams of renewal. There was a solidness in a long tradition as well as mystery.

My story has its own steps and turns. It is unlikely that yours will resemble it. But I believe God works around the world and in countless church communities. And still I ask, as perhaps you do too, sometimes wistfully, in what sense is the God we love and the love God brings active among his people? What is the Holy Spirit still doing?

SHY OF CHURCH?

Some of us are shy, like Emily Dickinson, of church. In our post-pandemic heartscape, we might better understand how fears might keep a person back from community. But when Emily's family members and friends died, did she mourn more alone than she might have? I think we still feel the pandemic effects of events and opportunities for gathering cut off and shut down, and suspicions flaring as we all tried our best to cope with the threats and the restrictions. She stopped going, staying at home Sunday mornings to watch the extended family's children.

Emily found herself pulling in, pulling away, even if, as one scholar noted, "Her Bible shows extensive use, its condition so fragile that the library [housing it] carefully monitors its use."[12] She was surrounded by family in her household's quarters, corresponded tirelessly, cared deeply for those close by. But what might joining with others in worship have done for her relating to God? Might she have felt less alone in the world, especially when grief after grief piled on as she lost family members and friends?

A LIVING FLAME OF LOVE

When Jesus promised the Holy Spirit, he pledged it to his gathered followers. Individuals benefit, to be sure, but I see a promise fulfilled best when his disciples come together in any age. It's what some have called a *living* flame of love: less like a wet match and more like spontaneous combustion. Something mighty. Something filled with a community's energy.

The Spirit on the move, still breathing and blowing, helps us live with power beyond our own. And an advocate like the Holy Spirit stirs up the gifts of others to serve, help, and teach. That's why the New Testament speaks so regularly about grace-gifts. No one has in himself or herself all the gifts; we need the complementing presence of them all. And then, when we meet, others might also find hope in the hard and harsh moments, not just the ones giddy with spiritual delight.

An advocate like the Holy Spirit stirs up the gifts of others to serve, help, and teach.

For the Spirit can visit us not just for our own benefit but for the good of others. Someone might need guidance or teaching. Another a listening ear. There are people longing to hear an invitation to God's grace in Christ and would that we could find the winsomeness and words to share it, to tell it abroad. "I have felt this in conversations specially visited by God," wrote author and editor Paul Pastor, "in teaching classes, in (once or twice) leading a gathering in prayer or worship."

The settings have varied. But he recalled moments where he "felt most in tune with the Spirit's will and voice, moments . . . that I (as Peter said) was being 'carried along' by the Spirit, the mode or method or language used as a means truly mattered very little to me. . . . The point of it all was that the Spirit wished to do something with words, in my life or another's, and he lit me or another on fire to be his voice. It is a feeling not quickly forgotten."[13]

Church becomes a kind of laboratory where we practice our gifts and graces, and the Spirit meets us there to help us along.

When teaching or preaching, or doing pretty much anything in front of people, I can obsess with the best of them. Will they even show up to listen? Or will this turn into a free nap session, a time to update their grocery list? Childhood insecurities sometimes stick with us throughout life.

I can also attest that God can take over that littleness and feebleness. I cease worrying about saying everything just so. I stop being aware of *myself*, my communication skills. I become aware of *God* in the room. I recall that the Holy Spirit has something to say. God in Christ is here, offering help and guidance. And the goal becomes getting out of the way and letting God do or say something through me, through us. Whether preaching before three or four at a chapel Eucharist midweek or preaching before three or four hundred on

Sunday morning for a cathedral service, I have found something happens that doesn't just hinge on me.

Whatever our setting might be, it's not about just you and me, thank goodness. It's the living, breathing Spirit who matters—the wind that through the ages has blown time and again through the paltriest speech and most mediocre talents. Even as a young person, I could sense its moving when I met with Brandt, and when I sat out the ocean baptism too. The Spirit, delighting with Father and Son, working indivisibly, can touch and move those he gladly tries to reach and enlist. And, as we will see, nothing less than God's Spirit can lead us to those who need, in turn, his overflowing help.

TEN

WHERE WILL THE SPIRIT LEAD US?

Hope does not put us to shame, because God's love has been poured out into our hearts through the Holy Spirit, who has been given to us.

—Romans 5:5

Blessed are those whose strength is in you [O God],
whose hearts are set on pilgrimage. . . .
They go from strength to strength,
till each appears before God in Zion.

—Psalm 84:5, 7

KEEPSAKES FROM OUR GROWING-UP YEARS OFTEN STIR something in us—reminders of losses or joys. One of mine from my childhood home is an antique mahogany Seth Thomas mantel clock. Its solid wood and old-fashioned workings make it sturdier than modern versions, but otherwise, it's nothing special—except to me. It sits above me on a high bookshelf in my study while I write. Part of its significance comes from the fact that it's one of just a few mementos I have from the house.

Growing up, I listened for its hourly chime. I liked the clock's early twentieth-century origin, an era when clocks had intricate mechanics and richly grained wood, not backlit digital numbers. Some years ago it stopped telling time; its chime-bell hammer's coiled spring held unreleased energy.

Between my mom's encroaching dementia, my living thousands of miles away, and the span of estrangement that still sometimes made communication with my family difficult, most of my parents' belongings were sold in an estate sale before I'd had a chance to consider what else I might retrieve.

So, while relatively small, the clock has a large place as a reminder of both happy times and harder moments. There were those years when I braved my parents' rejection of me, their threats to withhold any parental blessing of my life. With the patient passing of time, eventual reconciliation came, and the clock finally moved from their household to mine, to reside with a family formed at first against their hopes.

Our movement through life, of course, involves more than the measured ticking of any timepiece or the haptics of our smartphone timers. Time brings change—sometimes pain and hardship; sometimes the joy of new steps, like the new domestic life I forged with Jill, even with the emotional costs.

Our best spiritual traditions remind us that eternity has to do with the everyday, the infinite with this instant. If God holds us as his beloved in any real sense, it will be in the strokes and ticking minutes of daily life. My clock's Gothic arch comes to a peak like a cathedral window, as though pointing to the one who is above time—my time—while residing within it: a loving presence beyond our movements, not limited by the hands on a dial or figures on a smartwatch.

And much of what happens lies beyond our management or prediction. "The wind blows wherever it pleases," Jesus said of the Holy Spirit, making clear how God moves in ways we cannot direct or oversee.[1] Such a prospect unsettles us and excites us, both a challenge to complacency and the possibility of wild hopes. It adds an element of adventure to a life buoyed by the Holy Spirit. A bit of risk. And mystery.

God moves in a mysterious way,
His wonders to perform.
He plants his footsteps in the sea
And rides upon the storm.[2]

Much of our praying and living happens in the in-between: between daily struggles and eternal hope, between the brokenness of the world and the promise of healing, between human weakness and redemption. Human life in the Bible begins in a garden but sees the first residents driven out. It's no surprise we stumble, feel the urge to hide, or sit in the dark as the clock chimes until the coming light of dawn. Sometimes we long for the love we've given to be returned, and the nights involve restless, fitful waiting.

We see the way the world, too, "the whole creation," as Paul the apostle later described it, groans "as in the pains of childbirth right up to the present time."[3] The world longs for a postponed love and harmony. Those aching pangs erupt from our times' divisions and polarizing, injustices that seem to go unchallenged, and the apparent flourishing of those who hurt others and do evil. "How long, O Lord?" becomes a common biblical refrain.

In our weary waiting, it is tempting to reach for distractions—more things to buy, more noise online, even more spiritual "highs" to make us feel better.

And yet, there are moments when the ache itself becomes a kind of gift. When we recognize that the deep dissatisfaction points to something beyond what we can produce or control. The fractures in our world—and in us—become reminders of a longing for restoration that only God can bring. Paul reminded us that even our wordless groans become prayer, joined by the Spirit who intercedes for us. That is where hope takes root: not in our ability to explain or fix everything but in God's presence with us in the groaning, carrying us toward renewal.

LIVING IN THE IN-BETWEEN

How does the Holy Spirit—and for that matter, the whole fellowship of the Three—show us how to pray in this big in-between, the moments between the catastrophe human life can be and the making safe? How do we keep in our line of sight the Great God who calls us beloved? Who constantly wants good for the world?

I helped lead a group from a church I served on a trip to South Africa. We partnered with a sister congregation, St. Thomas Anglican Church in Kagiso, near Johannesburg. We had some projects related to housing and gardening, but mostly we came to see, learn, and be present. I had heard from others who had gone on a similar trip that I would witness the country's majestic beauty as well as stubborn signs of heartache and poverty. But I didn't realize how much what I saw would change my praying. I brought home new soberness, new urgency. Do you recall a time when you witnessed something particularly hard and hopeful, something that made you more urgent to see God's restoring work be done?

Our time began with lots of hugging. Early on our hosts at the partner church feted us with a breakfast reception. The people showered us with a love perhaps we did not yet quite deserve.

We helped plant a vegetable garden at a school for children of a nearby shantytown—simple enough, and rewarding. Another day we lent our sweat and muscle to build a wood-frame-and-tin-wall house for a family connected to our partner church. They had just lost their rickety home in a windstorm, and I will never forget the grandmother, as the walls were hoisted up, lifting her hands to Jesus with tears of thanks. Her daughter told us later that when evening rain came the night of our visit, they sang hymns of thanks, for the water could no longer leak through.

At museums and in conversations with our new friends we learned about apartheid, the oppressive national system that fell in the 1990s. We visited Kliptown and Soul City, with crowded acres of shanties serviced only by poor water and sanitation.

The images I saw moved me. I remember a conversation with someone in ministry there doing great things. "What role does prayer play?" I asked. "It runs through all we do," he said. "Our knees are hungry for prayer." What an image! I know, given the oppressive poverty, that some of his prayers were groans. Life does drive you to your knees sometimes. I realized I wanted to give praying for the people of South Africa a larger place in my intercessions.

While I expected to glimpse the land's beauty and a people's unshakable Christian faith, I didn't expect that afternoon's emotional stun gun. What we saw in the shantytown's rampant poverty rocked us back on our souls' heels and drove us to wonder about God's provision amid the people's suffering.

But I will never forget the congregation's worship! Our senses were filled. The ancient liturgy, not greatly different from ours in the States, combined with throbbing African percussion and electric bass, body-swaying hymns, and clouds of incense. "You gave us a great gift in your worship," I told the congregation toward the end of our time, "your vibrancy, your life, your faith, your love."

We learned from those who discovered the trustworthiness of God in the crucible of their struggle. They had been loved by God so vividly, even in the worst moments of oppression, that their affection spilled out into the lives of those around them—into our lives. I can barely fathom the patient waiting required of them, and yet they stayed faithful. Nothing shook their hope.

The night before I left, a friend and I were talking to our host in Soweto, George Punwhyo: He had seen suffering and, as a child and youth, bloodshed in the struggle against apartheid. He remembered well the protests in the streets and the violent attempts at suppression from the police. One of the protests was met with firepower that killed almost two hundred and injured a thousand.

He grew reflective one moment and said, "I don't know the depths of God, but I have seen his wonders. I have seen what he has done for me." Through hardship and setback, he sensed that God's purposes could not be thwarted. Such glimpses can keep us turning toward the God of consolation and help.

PRAYER AS PROTEST

We sometimes envision that the Spirit will suffuse our prayers with peace. And there is a peace that passes understanding. But the Spirit also stirs in another way. "Prayer," wrote Professor George Hendry, "is a form of protest with God against reality." To fold our hands in prayer, kneel in obedience, or lift up our arms in reverence is also a kind of uprising against the world as it is. Or perhaps it's gentler than that.

I love how Ellis Peters, in her medieval whodunit *A Morbid Taste for Bones*, paints a scene of Brother Cadfael's simple asking prayer: "He prayed as he breathed, forming no words and making no specific requests, only holding in his heart, like broken birds in cupped hands, all those people who were in stress or grief."[4]

Whether fierce or gentle, prayer enlists us through the Spirit in God's purposes through time. Sometimes we feel tempted to see intercession to God on behalf of others' needs as somehow intruding on God's doings, his privacy. That sentiment even sounds noble and humble.

But such resignation flattens praying. It keeps us from regularity, much less persistence. And such a view contradicts dozens of Scripture passages that specifically call us to ask, to pray—and to ask regularly. Many of the words for prayer in the Bible pulsate with energy: They are compelling, active words like *beg*, *beseech*, *cry out*. "Ask, seek, knock," declared Jesus. And the Spirit, we recall, groans in and through our praying.

Whether fierce or gentle, prayer enlists us through the Spirit in God's purposes through time.

And we pray, as Paul urged, "in the Spirit on all occasions with all kinds of prayers and requests."[5] We let the Spirit sweep us up in the Trinity's march toward God's vision of what is to be. We stay alert to God's intended purposes. For, as Jason Byassee wrote, "God has not begrudged us knowledge of himself or hid himself in obscurity. No, God has lavishly poured himself out on us in creation and redemption," and signs of life and goodness and the foreshadowings of the restoration to come are signs of the Holy Spirit.[6]

ACTIVE PATIENCE

But we flag sometimes. Lose a vision. Then patience helps. When Tertullian (c. 160–240) and others of the church leaders spoke of

God's patient endurance using the Latin word *patientia*, they had in mind something more than our just sitting back. They meant enduring, bearing, and not losing heart when suffering. Patience can be wonderfully, energetically active. For it is a disposition born of love. God always is giving birth to the new thing to come. We find the unflappable patience possible only for the beloved of God.

For the creation still waits "with eager longing" for "the revealing of the children of God," as Paul rhapsodized in Romans 8.[7] We carry on in the span between the harrowing effects of the fall and the coming consummation and glory, piecing together words, sighs, tears, and shouts as best we know. We await a new creation—God's immense reordering. For we have what we need to look ahead.

And to know where we are going, we recall where we come from. The long, rich story that precedes us and guides our future. The God of Abraham became the God of Jesus Christ and the reigning Lord of the earth. God promised to empower Abraham's descendants—a small and seemingly insignificant people—to transform the world. We remember visions like that found in Ephesians 1, where we see the world that God has destined to be. The church and its faith form part of the mystery working its way into what we attempt. The people of God through the ages wait in expectation. We know not only of the bondage of the old but also the new on the way.

In Jesus especially we see the kingdom breaking in all kinds of ways. We look at him and see the heart of the Creator. For now, in him, Israel's God was about to establish God's reign in world-shaking ways. "'The time has come,' [Jesus] said. 'The kingdom of God has come near. Repent and believe the good news!'"[8]

By the time we get to the Bible's last book, Revelation, with its sometimes-strange imagery, we get great encouragement for our prayers from this big in-between.

Its scenes intensify the possibilities. A prayer arc that begins in Adam's stuttering, tentative words climaxes. It bends toward an incomparably majestic end.

For in the visions in Revelation, God's invitation for dialogue with Adam and Eve and their descendants appears in more vivid strokes. Here the work of God in renewing creation in Christ and through Jesus' followers is amped up and blown wide open. God will finally have his fuller way with his beloved.

"The Spirit and the bride say, 'Come,'" John the Revelator is told.[9] That's Jesus and the Holy Spirit! Then John hears: "Yes, I am coming soon." And John fervently responded, in Scripture's last prayer, "Amen. Come, Lord Jesus!"[10] The last recorded biblical intercession! And here the longing overshadows any hesitancy. Now there's no holding back. *Come!* is no wary, halting prayer. It bursts forth in expectant asking. Praying takes on more exclamation points, expecting that God will answer with even more glory and presence. God in love will work even more restoration in the bent and broken. Here is longing for the full revelation, the full disclosure of God in Christ—the return in power and glory of the second Adam, to use the imagery of the apostle Paul—and Augustine.

Sometimes I get stuck. I'm better than Adam but not quite where the Revelator is, fresh from his vision of the resurrected Jesus. I carry on in the middle, between the Bible's two bookended prayers: "I was afraid!" and "Come, Lord Jesus!" I ask God to help my unbelief, my lack of trust in the thick of stressful days. Or I pray, as Jesus encouraged me to, for daily bread, unapologetic and urgent. I repeat Eastern Orthodoxy's great prayer echoing Mark's blind Bartimaeus: "Lord Jesus Christ, Son of God, have mercy on me." We invite the Holy Spirit to act and move too.

But lately I've started voicing this last, climactic prayer during the normal course of the day: "Come, Lord Jesus," especially when I'm staring down trouble. Or when I doomscroll and feel overwhelmed by the world's troubles. No less than the Holy Spirit and Jesus have invited us to do that.

The ending note of the Bible's final prayer carries even more weight. *Come*—not just to me, I also manage to pray, but also to the world. *Come again*, for the world's sake. Bring into fullness the re-creation in the mind of God from before time, before clock time or calendar time: *Come!* Come to make what is broken, incomplete, and far off whole and restored again. *Come* to the hard hit and bombed out. *Come* to my children and their children. *Come*—and then we name whatever the world's latest crises are. Knowing he's working to finish what he started, I can pray for God to bring his kingdom to consummation—its rightful conclusion, his intention for his beloved for all time.

So I find myself stretched to pray for a world where war or oppressive governments rip families apart. A world where unsuspecting young people endure unwanted sexual advances. A world where harrowing torture exists in the dark corners of modern dungeons. A world where some live in the shadows of unbelief.

Like John in Revelation, we ask in all kinds of urgent ways for the restoration of what has been forfeited. *Come, Lord Jesus*, we cry, as we continue to pray amid our soul's smallness, the sometimes-stale aftertaste of affluence, or the heartache of loss and death.

Sometimes the longing lifts beyond words. In our asking, words fall away, and halting inherited from the fall fades from memory. *Come*, we say to God, *so that your dream for your beloved continues to embolden our words—and renew our world.*

STILL IN THE PANGS

And we groan, in Paul's simple but memorable word, we mourn how cruel people can be to one another. We see evidence of our world's subjugation to what David Bentley Hart called the mutinous angelic and demonic forces.[11] God has won, but while the war has decisively turned, battles still rage on. Creation also knows something else. The forces of evil that resist God cannot defeat God.

In *The Lord of the Rings*, Sam Gamgee feels surprised to see his mentor, leader, and friend Gandalf show up when he thought him dead.

He stares with an open mouth, caught between bewilderment and joy, and says, "Gandalf! I thought you were dead! But then I thought I was dead myself. Is everything sad going to come untrue?"

"A great shadow has departed," said Gandalf. Then Tolkien wrote, "He laughed and the sound was like music, or water in a parched land; and as he listened the thought came to Sam that he had not heard laughter, the pure sound of merriment, for days upon days without count."[12]

Is everything sad going to come untrue? Yes.

God has done something amazing for us in Christ and sent the Holy Spirit to make Christ even more vividly, viscerally real. But while we have been adopted into God's loving family, the whole creation hasn't caught up yet. Which means the power of the Holy Spirit, the Spirit's work in history and the current moment, still needs attending. It needs our urgency. God's love for the world gives us our mission. And so, Jesus said as he approached his ascension, to go into all the world, making disciples, spreading the good news—using the most Trinitarian phrase you can imagine: In the name of the Father and of the Son and of the Holy Spirit.[13]

LOOKING UP, REACHING OUT

Intercessory prayer accompanies, then, not only the hard work, activism, and urgency; it also fits naturally into the movement of the Trinity's life. In intercessory prayer we participate fully in the overflow of divine relationality, the kind of interrelatedness Rowan mentioned to me in his Cambridge office. Does not the practice of asking prayer, which points our prayers toward *others*, take on new relevance when set against the backdrop of a God whose very being grows out of divine fellowship? No wonder Jesus rooted his followers' mission in the threefold name. That reality undergirds our working and praying and telling.

The vocabulary of location has great limitation, but it may still help to picture intercessory prayer as more than a vertical, upward glance. It is also a horizontal, sidelong opening of the eyes. We can understand, then, that it pours forth from God's love, already modeled among Father, Son, and Holy Spirit—the reality of the Trinity. That Presence, in turn, catches us up into its living, outward-reaching activity.

Intercessory prayer becomes an experience of participating in God's doings, then, because it is praying "in God," amid the loving interaction of Father, Son, and Holy Spirit. The praying has already begun; we don't start it up—we simply join in. As the letter to the Hebrews puts it, Christ "is able to save completely those who come to God through him, because he always lives to intercede for them."[14] This Son communicates eternally with the Father, not to plead our case as a lawyer before a stern and capricious Judge in heaven, but to draw others into the joyous conviction that they, too, are God's beloved.

And as we continue growing, will we not find the Three as close by and vibrant, moving the universe toward the Father's new creation vision and sweeping us up as he brings completion to the purposes of God in Christ? Ahead lies the transformation of all that is and the making right of what is not. Why, then, wouldn't hope be possible?

When Jill and I knew that we wanted to marry those decades ago, I came home from New Jersey for a short but difficult summer break from grad school. I tried, sometimes tearfully, to convince my parents to meet Jill—at least *that*.

During that visit, I often left the house to walk or run along the sandy Santa Monica beaches near our home. The Pacific Ocean extended past the western horizon, far beyond anything I could see. Above me, a wide sky opened, with an occasional sea gull soaring and cawing. Beyond me stretched a vast, comforting reality. I realized my life played out under a power not bound by immediate dilemmas and pain. God, in his creativity and patient love, would hold me up. The Spirit, who blows where he wills, would carry me forward—and our life together as a couple forward. When I came back to the house, I could see a future that I knew would include assurances I could count on and things I could not predict. Most of all, it would include a God, abounding in love, who would always be there to meet me wherever I went.

AFTERTHOUGHTS

Three-Personed Love

IN AN OLD PHOTO I RECENTLY FOUND WHILE JILL AND I were sorting boxes in our attic, I'm lying in the grass in our Virginia yard, holding our two-year-old son Abram—our firstborn—as high above me as my arms will reach. We are face-to-face, delighting in our play, some of his spittle, I suspect, drooling down as he laughs. Afternoon sunshine bathes the scene. I am grateful Jill snapped the photo.

And I smile when I look at it. Something in that unself-conscious delight captures some of what it means for relating to grow out of love and delight. It didn't matter much what I said. Abram didn't have many words at his young age. We just related. Our primary language in that scene of play was presence. Together, our primary reality was great, growing joy.

We've caught glimpses of the Trinity as a society of intimate relating and congenial collaborating. Glimmers, too, of a God who is not only personal but who overflows in love for us—for our world. I hope you have seen ways forward for yourself in all this. An invitation to greater intimacy. Sometimes a picture helps too.

An Anglican priest once told me how he sometimes prayed with help from the Trinity and a visual aid. He sat with a view of Andrei Rublev's renowned portrayal of the Holy Trinity. Of the three heavenly figures seated around a table—reminiscent of the angelic visitors that greeted Abraham in Genesis—he said, "When I pray with it, I picture God inviting me to the table to join in the fellowship."

Such an image provides a simple but profound picture of a God uncontainable in untold complexity and yet rich in relationship—rich toward us. Such is the mystery of the Trinity: not a mystery that baffles or confounds as much as one that calls forth reverent awe and growing expectancy that we, even in life's little moments, can share in that loving, wonder-filled communion. We ponder Jesus in his self-sacrificial love. And we experience, as we open our lives more fully to God, how the Spirit invites us over, catches us up, sweeps us out of our stuckness. In our lonely and broken world, we feel the mountain sunshine air of a warmly personal God in the Father, Son, and Holy Spirit—calling us, welcoming us.

Here, too, are mysteries, much like Gregory of Nazianzus discovered centuries ago, sharing his experience of wonder and delight: "No sooner do I conceive of the one than I am illumined by the splendor of the three; no sooner do I distinguish them than I am carried back to the one. When I think of anyone of the three I think of him as the whole, and my eyes are filled."[1]

Mystery, yes, but also clarity. Our imagination gets stretched and our awe swells again and again. And most of all, our love for the God of great love kindles and grows more radiant day by day.

ACKNOWLEDGMENTS

IT'S A MYTH: THE IMAGE OF THE SOLITARY WRITER, FAR from others, shut away in a lonely place, waiting for inspiration to strike.

At least for me, the more accurate counter-narrative is this: Creativity thrives in collaboration. As I've been writing, stronger insights and better expression have grown out of the loam of community and conversation. My writing deepened because of helpful feedback and vital support along the way.

And so, I want to thank several people.

Dr. Lauren Winner, whose workshops instilled in me a sense of what makes for better writing, early on encouraged my fledgling attempts to take on the Trinity as a major project.

Dr. Rowan Williams, who sat with me and my questions when I visited his study in England, showed kindness and great generosity with his time. His vigorous intellect, brought to bear as we talked, helped me believe I should keep going when initial efforts felt daunting and left me tentative.

I think of the folks, too many to name, who attended my classes at Trinity Episcopal Cathedral, Columbia; St. George's Episcopal Church, Nashville; and St. Bartholomew's Episcopal Church, Nashville. For their warm encouragement and good questions, I am grateful.

My retreat leading, speaking, and teaching at conference centers and churches around the country have reminded me how deeply I care about making complicated truths accessible, and I thank those attentive attendees.

Philip Yancey read a *very* rough early version and could not have been more encouraging, despite some of my still-forming thoughts and inelegant phrasing.

My writerly pen pal, David Bannon, a gifted writer and keen thinker, encouraged me often. So did Honey Davis and Garrett Ayers and Leigh Spruill.

My friend of a lifetime, Kevin Miller, has been faithful in prayer and full of encouragement. I am so grateful, more than I can say.

Conor Sweetman of *Inkwell* (formerly *Ekstasis*) has published several of my pieces, and I am grateful. Andy Patton and the great folks at the Rabbit Room in Nashville also published my work. Lil Copan helped me shape initial essay pieces into a much more cohesive and striking proposal to show to publishers.

My agent, Don Pape, of Pape Commons, has been delightful to work with—a writer's dream. My editor at Nelson Books, Paul Pastor, a fine writer himself, offered steady support and great insight, making this a much better book. Merry MacIvor was a keen-eyed and diligent copy editor. Janene MacIvor tended the book helpfully through final stages. Claire Drake and the marketing and sales team members at Nelson Books have also been wonderfully gracious.

On a more personal note: My son Micah Jones enlisted his professional consulting skills to bring clarity to his dad's calling as a writer and teacher.

My other son, Abram Kielsmeier-Jones, read almost all the chapters and offered invaluable critique and encouragement.

My wife, Jill Zook-Jones, contributed incredible insight to many of this book's themes. I cannot imagine life without her and our love and shared affection. Her wise comments over our decades of marriage have enriched my own thinking and praying, and more recently have helped me articulate what I wanted to say far better than I could have without her.

NOTES

Chapter 1: What If Love Ghosts Us?

1. Derek Thompson, "The Anti-Social Century," *The Atlantic*, January 8, 2025, https://www.theatlantic.com/magazine/archive/2025/02/american-loneliness-personality-politics/681091/.
2. Maggie Smith, *You Could Make This Place Beautiful* (One Signal/Atria, 2023), 177.
3. Smith, *You Could Make This Place Beautiful*, 18.
4. Frederick Buechner, "Love," Frederick Buechner Center, June 29, 2016, https://www.frederickbuechner.com/quote-of-the-day/2016/6/29/love.
5. Emily Dickinson, "We learned the Whole of Love," Fr531, *The Poems of Emily Dickinson: Reading Edition*, ed. R. W. Franklin (Belknap Press of Harvard University Press, 1998), 319.
6. Robert Letham, *The Holy Trinity* (P&R Publishing, 2019), 518.
7. Isaiah 55:12.
8. Genesis 1:26–28.
9. 2 Corinthians 13:13 NRSV.
10. Julian of Norwich, *Revelations of Divine Love*, trans. Barry Windeatt (Oxford University Press, 2015).
11. Catherine of Siena, *The Dialogue of Divine Providence*, trans. Suzanne Noffke, OP (Paulist Press, 1980), 167.
12. Fleming Rutledge, *The Crucifixion: Understanding the Death of Jesus Christ* (Eerdmans, 2015), 38.
13. Charles Williams, *Outlines of Romantic Theology*, ed. Alice Mary Hadfield (Eerdmans, 1990), 70.
14. Richard Lischer, *Our Hearts Are Restless* (Oxford University Press, 2023), 87.

15. Matthew 27:46.
16. James K. A. Smith, "I'm a Philosopher. We Can't Think Our Way out of This Mess," *The Christian Century*, March 10, 2021, https://www.christiancentury.org/article/how-my-mind-has-changed/i-m-philosopher-we-can-t-think-our-way-out-mess.
17. Ruth 1:16 NRSV.

Chapter 2: Who Ushered Me into This Messy Extravagance?

1. E. Lily Yu, *Break, Blow, Burn, and Make: A Writer's Thoughts on Creation* (Worthy Publishing, 2023), 3.
2. Psalm 139:13.
3. Martin Buber, quoted in David Bannon, "What Is a Miracle Anyway?," *Front Porch Republic*, May 13, 2025, https://www.frontporchrepublic.com/2025/05/what-is-a-miracle-anyway.
4. Brian Doyle, *One Long River of Song: Notes on Wonder* (Back Bay Books, 2019), 112.
5. Traditional African American spiritual, "Up Above My Head, I Hear Music in the Air."
6. C. S. Lewis, *Miracles* (HarperCollins, 2009), 117.
7. Anne Lamott, *Somehow: Thoughts on Love* (Riverhead Books, 2024), 2.
8. Psalm 22:10.
9. Psalm 139:13.
10. Gerard Manley Hopkins, "As Kingfishers Catch Fire," in *Poems and Prose* (Penguin Classics, 1985), 51.
11. Isaiah 55:8–9.
12. Augustine commented on Psalm 139 in his *Exposition on Psalm 139* (also known as *Sermon 35*), and in his *Confessions.*
13. Saint Augustine, *Confessions* (Oxford University Press, 1991), 8.
14. Martin Heidegger, as summarized in James K. A. Smith, *How to Inhabit Time* (Brazos, 2022), 32.
15. "Eastern Wisdom for Western Christians: Timothy Jones Interviews Rowan Williams," *The Christian Century*, May 4, 2022, https://www.christiancentury.org/article/interview/eastern-wisdom-western-christians.

Chapter 3: How Will Love Find Me in the Breathtaking and the Heartbreaking?

1. Marilynne Robinson, *The Givenness of Things* (Picador, 2016), 151.
2. Psalm 8:3–4 LEB.
3. Romans 1:20.
4. Psalm 19:1.

5. Brian Doyle, "Joyas Voladoras," *The American Scholar,* June 12, 2012, https://theamericanscholar.org/joyas-volardores/.
6. David Bannon, "Goethe's Grief," *Front Porch Republic*, July 14, 2025, https://www.frontporchrepublic.com/2025/07/goethes-grief/.
7. Augustine, *Confessions: A New Translation by Sarah Ruden* (Modern Library, 2018), 166.
8. Paul Mariani, *The Mystery of It All: The Mystery of Poetry in the Twilight of Modernity* (Paraclete Press, 2019), 52.
9. Makoto Fujimura, *Art and Faith: A Theology of Making* (Yale University Press, 2020), 18.
10. Genesis 1:2.
11. Vladimir Nabokov, *Speak, Memory: An Autobiography Revisited* (Vintage International, 1989), 3.
12. Flannery O'Connor, "A Good Man Is Hard to Find," in *Collected Works* (Library of America, 1988), 137.
13. Annie Dillard, *Pilgrim at Tinker Creek* (HarperCollins, 2007), 138–39.
14. Job 38:31–33.
15. Francis of Assisi, *The Canticle of Brother Sun*, in *Francis and Clare: The Complete Works*, trans. Regis J. Armstrong and Ignatius C. Brady (Paulist Press, 1982), 37.
16. Isaiah 17:10; Exodus 3; John 7:37–38; Exodus 19:4 NKJV.
17. Deuteronomy 32:18.
18. Michael Lloyd, *Café Theology* (Hodder & Stoughton, 2005), 17.
19. Julie Canlis, "Trinitarian Prayer," in *Essays on the Trinity*, ed. Lincoln Harvey (Cascade Books, 2018), 178.
20. Matt Canlis, *Backyard Pilgrim* (Godspeed Press, 2020), 18–19.
21. Eloise Wilkin, "Dear Father, Hear and Bless," in *Prayers for Children* (Simon & Schuster, 1942), 1.
22. 1 John 4:16.
23. Psalm 115:5–7.
24. Terrence Fretheim, *God and World in the Old Testament* (Abingdon, 2005), 18. It should be noted, though, that any talk of God's having feelings needs a healthy bit of cleansing of any human limitations. We don't want to limit God. God always "feels" in ways that are pure. We do so only sometimes.
25. Paul J. Pastor, *The Face of the Deep: Experiencing the Beautiful Mystery of Life with the Spirit* (David C. Cook, 2016), 34.
26. The technical word for this quality is *aseity*: God is fully God, in need of no help, dependent on no one or nothing, *a se* in Latin. It means "God is life in and of himself. He is independent of the created order, independent and self-existent." See Matthew Barrett, *Simply Trinity* (Baker, 2021), 319.
27. Isaiah 66:12–13.

28. Matthew 6:9 and Luke 11:2.
29. Mark 14:36 and Romans 8:15.
30. Julian of Norwich, *Revelations of Divine Love*, trans. Barry Windeatt (Oxford University Press, 2015), 132.
31. Richard Sibbes, *Works of Richard Sibbes*, 7 vols., Alexander B. Grosart, ed., (Edinburgh, 1862–1864; reprint ed., Edinburgh & Carlisle, PA: Banner of Truth, 1973–1982), 6:113, found at https://www.monergism.com/josiah's-reformation.
32. Ephesians 1:5 NRSV.
33. Luke 15.
34. James K. A. Smith, *On the Road with Saint Augustine* (Baker, 2019), 199.
35. Galatians 4:6 NRSV.

Chapter 4: What Happened, Unruly Heart?

1. Psalm 51:5.
2. Mockingbird, "Incurvatus in Se," *Glossary, Mockingbird Magazine*, accessed August 27, 2025, https://mbird.com/glossary/incurvatus-in-se/.
3. *The Book of Common Prayer* (Church Publishing, 1979), 478.
4. Romans 7:15.
5. Martin Luther, *Luther's Works*, vol. 25, ed. Jaroslav Pelikan (Fortress Press, 1963), 291–92, 345.
6. Jeremiah 17:9 ESV.
7. Francis Spufford, *Unapologetic: Why, Despite Everything, Christianity Can Still Make Surprising Emotional Sense* (HarperOne, 2013), 27.
8. James K. A. Smith, *On the Road with Saint Augustine* (Brazos Press, 2019), 66.
9. Genesis 3:9–10 NKJV.
10. Romans 8:22 NKJV.
11. Rowan Williams, *The Wound of Knowledge* (Darton, Longman and Todd, 1979), 90.
12. Saint Augustine, *Confessions,* trans. Henry Chadwick (Oxford University Press, 1991), 29.
13. Elizabeth Oldfield, *Fully Alive: Tending to the Soul in Turbulent Times* (Hodder & Stoughton, 2025), 144.
14. Oldfield, *Fully Alive,* 145.
15. Genesis 3:15.
16. James 4:1–2.
17. Tim Taylor, personal conversation with the author, August 2025.
18. *The Book of Common Prayer*, 218.
19. 2 Corinthians 13:14.
20. Origen, *De Principiis*, trans. Frederick Crombie, in *Ante-Nicene Fathers*,

vol. 4, ed. Alexander Roberts and James Donaldson (Christian Literature Publishing, 1885), 239–42.

21. C. S. Lewis, *Mere Christianity* (Collier/Macmillan, 1943), 38.
22. Chris Wheeler, "Blessing the Blasted New Year," *Mockingbird*, January 2, 2024, https://mbird.com/holidays/blessing-the-blasted-new-year/.
23. Kate Gaston, "The Martyr in the Mundane," *Ecstatic*, March 30, 2025, https://ekstasismagazine.substack.com/p/the-martyr-in-the-mundane.
24. David Zahl, *Seculosity: How Career, Parenting, Technology, Food, Politics, and Romans Became Our New Religion and What to Do About It* (Fortress Press, 2019), 67.
25. Julian of Norwich, *Revelations of Divine Love*, trans. Barry Windeatt (Oxford University Press, 2015).
26. Charlie Peacock, *Roots and Rhythm* (Eerdmans, 2025), 122.
27. Rowan Williams, interview with the author, *Christian Century*, May 4, 2022, https://www.christiancentury.org/article/interview/eastern-wisdom-western-christians.
28. Augustine, *Confessions*, trans. Henry Chadwick (Oxford University Press, 1991), I:1.
29. Augustine, *Homilies on the Gospel of John, 1–40*, ed. Edmund Hill (New City Press, 2009), 453.
30. Rowan Williams, *Ponder These Things: Praying with Icons of the Virgin* (Paraclete Press, 2002), 401, Kindle.

Chapter 5: Where Is a Haven for My Heart?

1. "Froggy Went a Courtin'," in *The Oxford Book of English Folk Songs*, ed. Philip Thorpe (Oxford University Press, 1976), 123.
2. Augustine, *Confessions*, 2.2.
3. 1 Timothy 6:16 NRSV.
4. Colossians 1:15.
5. Dallas Willard, *The Divine Conspiracy* (HarperSanFrancisco, 1998), 61.
6. Athanasius, *On the Incarnation*, in *A Select Library of the Nicene and Post-Nicene Fathers of the Christian Church*, ed. Philip Schaff, trans. Archibald Robertson, 2nd series, vol. 4 (Eerdmans, 1953), 20.
7. 1 John 4:14–16.
8. Mark 1:11.
9. Genesis 1:3, 24.
10. John 1:1.
11. John 1:14 NRSV.
12. Reynolds Price, "The Gospel According to Saint John," in *Incarnation*, ed. Alfred Corn (Viking Penguin, 1990), 72.
13. Julie Canlis, *A Theology of the Ordinary* (Godspeed Press, 2017), 28–29.

14. Abram Kielsmeier-Jones, "That One Time Jesus Burst into Tears," *Healing Pastors* (blog), April 23, 2025, https://healingpastors.substack.com/p/that-one-time-jesus-burst-into-tears.
15. Psalm 122:1 ESV.
16. N. T. Wright, "Where Heaven and Earth Meet: A Jesus-Centered Spirituality for Today," NTWright Online, https://www.ntwrightonline.org/wp-content/uploads/2022/08/Where-Heaven-and-Earth-Meet-PDF.pdf.
17. Irenaeus of Lyons, *Against Heresies,* https://ia904501.us.archive.org/11/items/SaintIrenaeusAgainstHeresiesComplete/Saint%20Irenaeus%20Against%20Heresies%20Complete.pdf.
18. "Te Deum laudamus," *The Book of Common Prayer,* 2016, https://www.bcponline.org/, 96.
19. Natalie Carnes, *Motherhood: A Confession* (Stanford University Press, 2020), 167, Kindle.
20. Julian of Norwich, *Revelations of Divine Love*, trans. Barry Windeatt (Oxford University Press, 2015), 76, 49, 43, and 45, respectively.
21. Julian of Norwich, *Revelations,* 77.
22. Barbara W. Tuchman, *A Distant Mirror: The Calamitous 14th Century* (Alfred A. Knopf, 1978), 92.
23. Julian of Norwich, *Revelations,* 115.
24. Julian of Norwich, *Revelations*, 47–48.
25. Athanasius of Alexandria, *On the Incarnation*, trans. and ed. Religious of the C. S. M. V. (St. Vladimir's Seminary Press, 1996), 43.

Chapter 6: Will Love Find and Mend Me?

1. Strahan Coleman, *Beholding: Deepening Our Experience in God* (NavPress, 2022), 9.
2. A sermon preached by Sarah Condon at St. Bartholomew's Episcopal Church, March 16, 2025, https://creators.spotify.com/pod/profile/st-bartholomews/episodes/March-16--2025--Sermon-by-Rev--Sarah-Condon-e37dd4v.
3. John Donne, introduction to *The Complete English Poems*, ed. A. J. Smith (Penguin, 2003).
4. Philip Yancey, *The Jesus I Never Knew* (Zondervan, 1995), 187.
5. Philippians 2:6–8.
6. E. Lily Yu, *Break, Blow, Burn, and Make: A Writer's Thoughts on Creation* (Worthy Publishing, 2023), 251.
7. Fleming Rutledge, *The Crucifixion: Understanding the Death of Jesus Christ* (Eerdmans, 2017), 181.

8. Anselm of Canterbury, quoted in Rutledge, *The Crucifixion: Understanding the Death of Jesus Christ* (Eerdmans, 2017), 149.
9. Fleming Rutledge, *The Seven Last Words from the Cross* (Eerdmans, 2004), 7–8.
10. C. S. Lewis, *Mere Christianity* (HarperOne, 2001), 57.
11. 1 Peter 3:18.
12. "The Esultet, or Easter Proclamation," in *The Book of Common Prayer* (Church Publishing, 1979), 286.
13. Jürgen Moltmann, *The Crucified God: The Cross of Christ as the Foundation and Criticism of Christian Theology*, trans. R. A. Wilson and John Bowden (Fortress Press, 1974), 143–44.
14. Matthew 27:46.
15. Psalm 22:3, 5.
16. "The Apostles' Creed," in *The Book of Common Prayer* (Church Publishing, 1979), 12.
17. John Donne, "Good Friday, 1613. Riding Westward," in *The Complete Poetry of John Donne*, ed. A. J. Smith (Penguin Classics, 2001), 427.
18. Thomas F. Torrance, *The Trinitarian Faith: The Evangelical Theology of the Ancient Catholic Church* (T&T Clark, 1991), 57.
19. 1 Peter 3:18.
20. For those really wanting to get technical, the word in the Greek is *homoousios*, and it mattered a great deal in the early church's debates.
21. Matthew 23:37.
22. John 13:1 NRSV.
23. John 1:1.
24. Michael Casey, *Toward God: The Ancient Wisdom of Western Prayer* (Triumph Books, 1996), 2.
25. Rowan Williams, *Resurrection: Interpreting the Easter Gospel* (Darton, Longman and Todd, 1982), 996, Kindle.
26. *The Book of Common Prayer* (Church Publishing, 1979), 292, 361–64, 369.

Chapter 7: How Will God Meet Me When Hope Wanes?

1. 1 Thessalonians 4:13.
2. Dylan Thomas, "Do Not Go Gentle into That Good Night," in *Collected Poems: 1934–1952* (New Directions, 1952), 128.
3. "If Death Is the End of You," a sermon preached at Church of the Savior, Wheaton, Illinois, February 15, 2025, https://friendsofthesavior.org/sermons/if-death-is-the-end-of-you.
4. Ernest Becker, *The Denial of Death* (The Free Press, 1973), 26.
5. Eberhard Arnold, "Life Is Eternal," in *Plough*, January 9, 2025, https://www.plough.com/en/topics/faith/devotional-reading/life-is-eternal.

6. 1 Corinthians 15:55–57.
7. Fleming Rutledge, *The Crucifixion: Understanding the Death of Jesus Christ* (Eerdmans, 2015), 511.
8. Timothy Jones, *Awake My Soul* (Doubleday, 1999).
9. Hebrews 13:14.
10. 2 Corinthians 4:18.
11. Romans 6:4.
12. Wendell Berry, *Leavings: Poems* (Counterpoint, 2009), 94.
13. Paul Pastor, *The Face of the Deep: Experiencing the Beautiful Mystery of Life with the Spirit* (David C. Cook, 2020), 31.
14. Romans 8:11.
15. Ephesians 1:19–20.
16. Matthew 25:40.
17. N. T. Wright, *Surprised by Hope: Rethinking Heaven, the Resurrection, and the Mission of the Church* (HarperOne, 2008), 208.
18. Helen H. Lemmel, "Turn Your Eyes upon Jesus," in *Turn Your Eyes upon Jesus* (British National Sunday School Union, 1922).
19. Lemmel, "Turn Your Eyes upon Jesus."

Chapter 8: What Is This Electrifying Love?

1. Song of Songs 6:3.
2. Timothy Jones, *The Art of Prayer: A Simple Guide to Conversation with God* (Ballantine, 1997; repr., WaterBrook, 2005).
3. Strahan Coleman, "Spiritual Dryness: The True Fire of Love," July 24, 2024, https://commonerscommunion.substack.com/p/spiritual-dryness-the-true-fire-of.
4. Rowan Williams, *On Christian Theology* (Blackwell, 2000), 107.
5. Romans 5:5, emphasis added.
6. Brennan Manning, *The Relentless Tenderness of Jesus* (Revell, 2004).
7. Ephesians 4:30.
8. John 14:28.
9. John 14–17.
10. Veli-Matti Kärkkäinen, *The Holy Spirit* (Westminster John Knox Press, 2012), 2.
11. Romans 8:28.
12. Romans 8:26–27.
13. Genesis 1:2 THE MESSAGE.
14. In the original language of the New Testament, the word *pneuma,* from which we get words like *pneumonia* or *pneumatic,* is genderless but personal. Traditional pronoun usage tends to he and him.

15. Sarah Ruden, *The Face of the Deep: A Translator on Beauty and Meaning in the Bible* (Pantheon, 2017), 42.
16. "The Nicene Creed," in *The Book of Common Prayer* (Church Publishing, 1979), 358.
17. John 6:63.
18. Clark Pinnock, *Flame of Love: A Theology of the Holy Spirit,* 2nd ed. (InterVarsity Press, 2022), 52.
19. 2 Samuel 23:2.
20. Psalm 51:11.
21. Isaiah 11:2–3.
22. Joel 2:28–29.
23. Matthew 1:18 NRSV.
24. 1 Peter 3:18.
25. Ephesians 1:19–20.
26. Jürgen Moltmann, *The Spirit of Life: A Universal Affirmation*, trans. Margaret Kohl (Fortress Press, 1992), 9.
27. John 14:25–26.
28. Romans 12; 1 Corinthians 12; Ephesians 4.
29. Pinnock, *Flame of Love*, 287.
30. Athanasius, quoted in Kevin Douglas Hill, *Athanasius and the Holy Spirit* (Fortress Press, 2016), 145.
31. Gregory of Nazianzus, quoted in Christopher Beeley, *Gregory of Nazianzus on the Trinity and the Knowledge of God* (Oxford University Press, 2008), 159.
32. Emily Dickinson, "Your thoughts don't have words every day," Fr1476, in The *Poems of Emily Dickinson: Reading Edition*, ed. R. W. Franklin (Belknap Press of Harvard University Press, 1998), 555.
33. Makoto Fujimura, *Art and Faith: A Theology of Making* (Yale University Press, 2020), 2.
34. Emily Dickinson, *The Letters of Emily Dickinson*, ed. Thomas H. Johnson and Theodora Ward, 3 vols. (Belknap Press of Harvard University press, 1958), 2:412.
35. Roger Lundin, *Emily Dickinson and the Art of Belief,* 2nd ed. (Eerdmans, 2004), 3.
36. Dickinson, "1695," in *The Poems of Emily Dickinson*, 695.
37. 1 Corinthians 14:14–15.
38. Elizabeth Oldfield, "Getting to the Real Stuff," *Mockingbird*, Spring 2025, https://mbird.com/shop/magazine/issue-26-the-holy-spirit/.
39. Ephesians 6:18.
40. Thomas Kelly, *A Testament of Devotion* (Harper & Row, 1941), 45.

Chapter 9: What Life Is Possible When Love Blossoms?

1. John 13.
2. Acts 2:42–46.
3. William Willimon, *Acts* (John Knox Press, 1988), 33.
4. Robert E. Webber, *The Divine Embrace* (Baker, 2006), 218.
5. Ecclesiastes 4:9–12.
6. Eugene Peterson, *The Wisdom of Each Other* (Zondervan, 1998), 49.
7. "But the fruit of the Spirit is love, joy, peace, forbearance, kindness, goodness, faithfulness, gentleness and self-control. Against such things there is no law" (Galatians 5:22–23).
8. Jeremy Begbie, *Abundantly More: The Theological Promise of the Arts in a Reductionist World* (Baker Academic, 2023), 210–11.
9. Augustine, *Expositions of the Psalms 33–50*, trans. María Boulding, OSB, ed. John E. Rotelle, OSA, *The Works of Saint Augustine: A Translation for the 21st Century* III/16 (New City Press, 2000), 10–11.
10. Augustine, *Expositions*, 10–11.
11. Begbie, *Abundantly More*, 211.
12. Dorothy Huff Oberhaus, *Emily Dickinson's Fascicles* (Pennsylvania State University Press, 1995), 3–4.
13. Paul Pastor, *The Face of the Deep: Experiencing the Beautiful Mystery of Life with the Spirit* (David C. Cook, 2016), 211.

Chapter 10: Where Will the Spirit Lead Us?

1. John 3:8.
2. William Cowper, "God Moves in a Mysterious Way," in *Olney Hymns, in Three Books*, book 1 (Oliver, 1779), hymn 68.
3. Romans 8:22.
4. Ellis Peters, *A Morbid Taste for Bones* (Macmillan, 1977), 121.
5. Ephesians 6:18.
6. Jason Byassee, *Trinity: The God We Don't Know* (Abingdon, 2015), 33.
7. Romans 8:19 NRSV.
8. Mark 1:15.
9. Revelation 22:17.
10. Revelation 22:20.
11. David Bently Hart, *The Doors of the Sea: Where Was God in the Tsunami?* (Eerdmans, 2005), 62.
12. J. R. R. Tolkien, *The Return of the King: Being the Third Part of the Lord of the Rings* (Houghton Mifflin, 1955), 100–101.
13. Matthew 28:19.
14. Hebrews 7:25.

Afterthoughts

1. Gregory of Nazianzus, Oration 40:41, https://www.newadvent.org/fathers/310240.htm. See also Justin Taylor, "The Trinity: Gregory of Nazianzus on the Three and the One," Gospel Coalition, February 25, 2021, https://www.thegospelcoalition.org/blogs/justin-taylor/the-trinity-gregory-of-nazianzus-on-the-three-and-the-one/.

ABOUT THE AUTHOR

TIMOTHY JONES is a pastor and author known for helping people uncover greater warmth and depth in their relationship with God. His books include *Awake My Soul: Practical Spirituality for Busy People*; *The Art of Prayer*; and *Celebration of Angels*. Tim enjoys good stories and playing old-time banjo music. He lives near Nashville with his wife, Jill.